Growing in CHRiST®

Early Childhood
Teacher Guide

CONCORDIA PUBLISHING HOUSE · SAINT LOUIS

God Sends His Son
to Save Us

NEW TESTAMENT 1

Lessons 1, 2, 4, 6 & 11 written by Deanna Sandcork and Lorraine Groth

Lessons 3, 7 & 8 written by Jessamyn Pekari and Lorraine Groth

Lesson 5 written by Christine Behnke and Lorraine Groth

Lesson 9, 10, 12 & 13 written by Marlene Krohse and Lorraine Groth

Edited by Lorraine Groth

Growing in Christ® is published by Concordia Publishing House. Your comments and suggestions concerning this material are appreciated. E-mail us at sundayschool@cph.org.

Contents

Introduction

For the New User

Early Childhood is a nonreader level for children in preschool and kindergarten. It includes a Teacher Guide, Teacher Tools (for teachers), and Student Pack (for the children).

Features of the Teacher Guide

- Easy-to-use, four-step weekly lesson plans
- A weekly Bible study on the first page of each lesson to help the teacher prepare
- Reproducible student Activity Page in each lesson
- Age-appropriate ways to teach the Bible story and apply it to young lives
- Themed snack suggestions in each lesson
- Songs, wiggles-out rhymes, and ways to involve children in active learning
- Quarterly supply list at the back of the book
- Perforated pages to make team teaching or small-group/large-group teaching easier

Teacher Tools

This packet provides the following resources for effective teaching:

- **Posters** (teaching aids and Bible story posters)
- **Storytelling Figures** (four pages of figures for telling the Bible stories)
- **Bible Story Background Tent** (two background scenes to use with the storytelling figures)
- **Attendance chart**
- **CD** (recordings of hymns, songs, Bible Words, and Bible stories; melody-line scores for all music on the CD, Activity Pages, Resource Pages, and a list of student Bible Words in PDF format; and song lyrics in RTF format)

Student Pack

You will need one for each child. This packet includes the following materials:

- **Student Book** (Lesson Leaflets, Craft Pages, and a list of the Bible Words at the back of the book to send home with the children)
- **Sticker Pages** (three pages with perforated sections for each lesson)
- **CD** (songs, hymns, catechism songs, and Bible memory words songs)

Additional Teaching Helps

Call 1-800-325-3040 for subscription and cost information to order the following helps:

- *Little Ones Sing Praise* (*LOSP*) songbook
- *Sing & Wonder* (*S&W*) songbook
- *Wiggle & Wonder: Bible Story Rhymes and Finger Plays* (*W&W*)
- *Happy Times*, a magazine for young children
- **Puppets**—find an assortment of fun puppets online at cph.org; Jelly can be used interchangeably with Sprout
- **Restickable glue stick**—to allow for repeat use in attaching storytelling figures to backgrounds (order online or at cph.org, or find in the office supply section of your local discount store)
- **Church Year Worship Kit**—a great resource for teaching children about the Church Year (includes a Leader Guide, an altar poster with paraments and more, prayer posters, and a CD)

Early Childhood Format

Young children need a safe environment with predictable routines and the same caring adults each week to feel secure. For this reason, we recommend letting the children learn in their own space, separate from the rest of your program, where they can relax, play, and engage in age-appropriate activities.

You can still make choices in how you organize your Sunday School session and space. Choose the option that works best for your program or tailor the material to work for your local situation.

Option 1

This format works well if you have just one group of children with one teacher (or a teacher and helper). It is a traditional self-contained classroom, where the teacher does all the activities with the whole group of children. If this format suits you, begin with the Welcome Time learning activities and work through the lesson as it is written, adapting the materials to fit your time frame and children's needs. Encourage parents to do the Activity Page with their child before they leave. This helps children transition into the classroom more easily. It also gives parents a better understanding of what the lesson will be about so they can talk later with their child about what he or she learned.

Make copies of the Activity Page Fun (available on the Teacher CD) before class so each parent or helper has one. Set these out with copies of the designated Activity Page and the other supplies they'll need.

If your class session is under an hour, omit the Welcome activities and start with the Opening Ritual or Bible story.

Option 2

If you have a large number of children in your early childhood program, try a large-group, small-group format.

In this approach, children gather in their own classrooms or designated space to do the Welcome Time learning activities. These activities serve two purposes: they help children transition into the classroom, and they activate prior knowledge, building interest and readiness for what children will learn in the lesson. Encourage parents to do the Activity Page with their child during this time before going to their own Bible study session.

When it is time to begin, all children in your early childhood program gather with their teachers in one location for the opening worship ("Gathering in God's Name"). Stay in this location to have a teacher tell the Bible story to the whole group, or have children go back to their own classrooms again for the Bible story ("God Speaks"), told by their classroom teacher.

The "We Live" life-application activities can be done in two ways. Teachers can do these activities in their classroom with their small group of children. Or you can set up each activity as a station. Children divide into small groups and rotate to these stations or sites. Then all preschoolers through kindergartners come back together again for the closing.

Abbreviations

LSB = Lutheran Service Book (Concordia Publishing House, 2006)

LOSP = Little Ones Sing Praise (Concordia Publishing House, 1989)

W&W = Wiggle & Wonder (Concordia Publishing House, 2012)

S&W = Sing & Wonder (Concordia Publishing House, 2015)

TG = Teacher Guide

Name Tags

Copy the dove and shell (or one of the other symbols). Let children choose one. Help them write their name on it. Punch a hole in the top and string with yarn to wear. The dove and shell remind us that God the Holy Spirit makes us His children through Baptism and His Word.

Mobile

Make copies of the symbols on the next page. Give children crayons or markers to color them. Provide glue and tactile components to add to each symbol, such as cotton balls (for cloud), non-metallic glitter (for butterfly), a Jesus sticker (for heart), and narrow ribbon (for cross).

Cut them out, and punch a hole in the top of each one. Use varying lengths of yarn to fasten the cutouts to a wire coat hanger, or cut paper plates in half and attach the cutouts to the flat edge. Ask children to name the shapes. Point out that the heart can remind us of God's love, the cross tells us that Jesus died for us, the butterfly reminds us that He rose again on Easter, and the cloud helps us remember that we will live in heaven someday.

8

Preparing the Lesson

The Birth of John Foretold

Luke 1:5–25

Key Point

God promised to send John to prepare sinners to receive the Savior. Through His Word, God calls us to repent and declares us righteous because of Jesus.

Law/**Gospel**

I sin when I doubt God's Word and promises. **God sent His Son to forgive my sin and works through His Word and Sacraments to give me faith to believe and to strengthen my trust in Him.**

Context

God set up the regulations for the tabernacle, and later the temple, in order to establish and maintain His people. God is merciful in providing sacrifices to cleanse that which is unclean and make holy that which is common.

Commentary

God promises to make His people a holy nation, a kingdom of priests. Zechariah and his fellow priests followed all the temple regulations with the result that God's people were taught right from wrong and that God loves and forgives them.

The name *Zechariah* means "God will remember." God remembered His people by sending His holy messenger Gabriel to Zechariah to announce the birth of John, the forerunner and relative of Jesus. Zechariah was not only rightfully gripped with fear, but he also doubted God's message.

Would we not also doubt? After all, God had not sent a prophet or an angel for centuries. Yet God forgave Zechariah's doubting and gave him the cross of muteness to bear as a sign of the coming blessing of John, whose name means "the Lord is gracious and moved to pity."

Even when we bear our crosses, they testify to Christ. In this world or in the next, He gives us so much joy that all suffering for His sake will be forgotten, swallowed up in His love and abundant gifts.

God knows us, loves us, and desires to save us, even before we are born. God does not forgive us because of our worldly righteousness, but because Jesus exchanged His perfect righteousness for our deep and abiding sin when He was killed on the cross in our place. All those who speak the truth of God's love speak about the person and work of Jesus for us. Our human thoughts and frailties do not limit God's love. Nothing is impossible with God.

To hear an in-depth discussion of this Bible account, visit cph.org/podcast and listen to our Seeds of Faith podcast each week.

Lesson 1
The Birth of John Foretold
Luke 1:5–25

Connections

Bible Words
The LORD will do the thing that He has promised.
2 Kings 20:9

Faith Word
Promise

Hymn
My Soul Rejoices
(*LSB* 933; CD 3)

Catechism
Apostles' Creed: First and Second Articles

Take-Home Point
God keeps all His promises.

1 Opening (15 minutes)

Welcome Time

What you do: Before class, set up two activity areas. In one, put out copies of Activity Page 1, stickers (Sticker Page), and crayons. Copy Activity Page Fun (below and on CD) for parents or classroom helpers. Adjust talk as necessary.

In the other activity area, set out a baby bottle, rattle, bib, or pictures of these items in a paper bag. In a second bag, place an unbreakable angel figure.

Play the CD from your Teacher Tools. As the children arrive, greet each one. Give them a sticker to put on the attendance chart and a name tag to wear, or set out supplies for them to make name tags.

Say Hi, [Louisa]. I'm glad to see you! I wonder . . . do you like to get letters or packages in the mail? Whom do you get them from? Today, you'll hear about a time God sent a message to someone in a special way.

Direct the children to the tables where you have the activities. Encourage parents or caregivers to stay and do the welcome activity with their child.

Activity Page Fun Get a copy of Activity Page 1 and stickers. Show the page to your child.

Ask Who are all these people? What do they do for us? Talk about how the people are messengers who bring mail or packages or news. Have your child add stickers to the people who deliver the item represented by the sticker.

Say Today, you will hear about a man who received good news. It didn't come in the mail, though. You'll have to listen to the Bible story to find out how the message was delivered.

MATERIALS NEEDED

1 Opening	2 God Speaks	3 We Live	4 Closing
Teacher Tools Attendance chart & CD	**Teacher Tools** Poster A	**Student Pack** Craft Page 1	**Teacher Tools** CD
Student Pack Attendance sticker Activity Page stickers	**Student Pack** Craft Page 1 Lesson Leaflet 1 Sticker	**Other Supplies** Sprout or another puppet Paper cups Angel-shaped sugar cookies Angel stamps or cookie cutters Paper Plus supplies (optional)	**Student Pack** Student CDs List of Bible Words
Other Supplies Activity Page 1 (TG) Paper bags, baby items & angel Name tags Resource Page 1 (TG)	**Other Supplies** Sprout or another puppet Play dough & craft sticks (optional) Incense or a candle (optional) Garland or bathrobe (optional)		**Other Supplies** Ribbon or crepe paper Take-home items

Active Learning Let the children take the baby items out of the first bag and look at them.

Ask **Who uses things like this? Could someone big like you use them? Whom would you give these things to?** Discuss how a baby uses these things. Open the second bag and talk about what is inside.

What is this? An angel. I wonder . . . how do things for a baby and an angel go together? We'll find out in our Bible story today!

Use your classroom signal to let the children know it's time to clean up and gather for circle time. Sing a cleanup song (Resource Page 1).

Say **Pretend there is a baby sleeping in this room. Everyone tiptoe to the rug quietly so we won't wake the baby.**

Gathering in God's Name

What you do: Gather the children, and begin with this opening. To teach about the Church Year, use the materials in the Church Year Worship Kit (see the introduction for more information).

Sing "Our Church Family" (*LOSP*, p. 11; CD 15) or another opening song

Say **Today, we're going to hear about a promise God made.**

Invite the children to say the Invocation and Amen with you. Tell them "Amen" is the special word they get to say at the end of prayers, hymns, and parts of the church service.

Begin **In the name of the Father and of the Son and of the Holy Spirit. Amen.**

Offering Have a child bring the offering basket forward. Sing an offering song.

Pray **Thank You, God, for everything,* especially our Savior, Jesus.* Help us to listen and learn today.* Bless our time together, we pray.* Amen.***

*Have children echo each phrase after the asterisk.

Celebrate Birthdays, Baptism birthdays, and special occasions

2 God Speaks (20 minutes)

Story Clue

What you do: Use Sprout or another puppet.

Say **Boys and girls, we have a special friend with us today.** Show Sprout. **His name is Sprout! Let's welcome him by saying hello.** Do this.

Sprout: (*Sounding grumpy*) Hi.

Teacher: What's wrong, Sprout? You don't sound too happy this morning.

Sprout: I'm not! I really wanted to go with Lily to the store today. Yesterday, she *promised* that I could go with her, but today, she said I couldn't go. That's not fair!

Teacher: Oh, you're unhappy because your cousin didn't keep her promise.

Sprout: Right! And she isn't the only one who doesn't keep promises. Last week, my friend promised I could play at his house; then he didn't let me.

Teacher: Well, Sprout, sometimes boys and girls and even grown-ups make promises they can't keep. Have you ever made a promise you didn't keep?

Sprout: No! I keep all my promises!

Teacher: Really? Have you ever promised to pick up your toys, but instead of doing that, you kept on playing? Have you ever promised to go to bed quietly, but instead of doing that, you made a fuss?

Sprout: Um, maybe . . .

Teacher: That's what I thought! I don't keep all my promises either, Sprout, but I know someone who does—God! Today, we'll hear about a promise God made to a man named Zechariah. Zechariah didn't believe God would keep His promise either. But God always keeps His promises.

Bible Story Time

What you do: If you have an extra Craft Page 1, cut out and tape the Zechariah and Elizabeth figures to craft sticks and place them in lumps of play dough to make them into story puppets. Cover the angel on Poster A with a piece of paper. If it is not against your fire code, burn incense or light a candle where indicated. Have your Bible open, and tell children this is a true story from God's Word.

Say **The Bible tells us that there was a man named Zechariah who loved God very much.** Hold up the Zechariah puppet, or point to Zechariah on Poster A. **He was married to a woman named Elizabeth, but they had no children.** Show Elizabeth puppet. **They both wanted a baby very much.**

Zechariah worked in God's house, the temple. Point to Zechariah on Poster A. **One day, Zechariah went into a special holy place in God's house to burn incense and to pray.** Explain what incense is; then light it or a candle. **All of a sudden, the angel Gabriel stood by him.** Remove paper to reveal the angel. **Zechariah had never seen an angel before. He was afraid! Show me on your face what it looks like to be afraid.** Model look.

The angel said, "Don't be afraid. I have a message for you. I bring you good news from God! Your wife, Elizabeth, is going to have a baby boy. His name will be John, and he will grow up to do special work. God wants him to tell people that Jesus is coming to be their Savior."

Zechariah and Elizabeth had wanted a baby for many years, but Zechariah thought they were too old to have one now. So, he didn't believe the angel. Zechariah asked, "How can this happen?"

The angel told him, "I am Gabriel. God sent me to tell you this good news. But since you do not believe me, you won't be able to talk until the baby is born."

The people outside were waiting for Zechariah. When he came out, he couldn't talk to them—not even one word. Shake head no. **Zechariah could only make signs with his hands. The people knew something special must have happened to Zechariah. Then Zechariah went back inside. He finished his time of serving in the temple and went home to Elizabeth.** Show Zechariah and Elizabeth puppets.

Later, Elizabeth found out that she was going to have a baby. How

happy Zechariah and Elizabeth were! God had kept His promise!

God sent the angel Gabriel to give Zechariah a good-news message. God loves us and gives us many promises in His Word. He wants us to trust Him to keep His promises. With God, all things are possible.

Bible Story Review

What you do: Show Poster A. Use the questions to review the story and check for understanding. Then hand out Lesson Leaflet 1, the baby John stickers, and crayons. For an active review, provide simple props (e.g., a bathrobe and garland for a halo) to use in acting out the story.

Ask **What is the angel telling Zechariah?** He tells him not to be afraid. God has sent him to tell Zechariah that he and Elizabeth will have a baby.

What happened to Zechariah when he didn't believe the angel? He couldn't talk.

Will God keep His promise to Zechariah? Yes.

Then tell children to place a finger on each of the pictures in the sidebar as you say the word describing the picture. Read from top to bottom.

Ask **What did God promise to give Zechariah?** A baby. **Circle the picture that shows God's promise to Zechariah.**

After children circle the baby, have them color the pictures, then trace the dots on the Bible as you talk about where we hear God's promises for us. Give children a sticker of baby John to put on the photo page on side 2 of the leaflet. Talk about what God promised.

Do Act out the story together. Assign the parts of Zechariah, the angel, Elizabeth, and the waiting crowd. Turn a desk or table into the altar. Direct the action as the children reenact the story. Use a tablet device to record the action. Play it in class for the children. Then send it to parents to watch this week.

Great Idea!

Bible Words

What you do: Do the action poem with the children to introduce the Bible Words. Read the verse from 2 Kings 20:9 in your Bible.

Say **I open my Bible book up wide**
Hold your hands, palms together, in front of you.
And read the words that are inside.
Open your hands like an open book.

The Bible says, "The Lord will do the thing that He has promised." Elizabeth and Zechariah were so old that they didn't think they could have a baby. But God sent an angel with good news for Zechariah. The angel told him that he and his wife would have a baby.

Ask **Will God keep His promise? Yes!** Read from Bible: **"The Lord will do the thing that He has promised." Elizabeth would have a baby.**

Now say, "Good News! Good News!" with me. Then we'll clap and say our Bible Words.

Good News! Clap. Clap. **Good News!** Clap. Clap.
"The Lord will do the thing that He has promised."

③ We Live (15 minutes)

Use these activities to help the children grow in their understanding of what the Bible story means for their lives. Choose the ones that work best with your class.

Growing through God's Word

What you do: Bring Sprout back. Have CD cued to track 10 for song.

Say **Our God is great! He gives us many promises in His Word. And He always keeps His promises to us.** Talk about some of God's promises (e.g., to hear our prayers and care for us). **Even though Zechariah didn't believe the angel at first, God still loved Zechariah and forgave him.**

God wants us to trust Him to keep His promises. Sometimes, though, we don't believe God's promises either, or we forget what He tells us. When we don't trust God, we are sinning. But God still loves us. He sent Jesus to die on the cross to pay for our sins. He forgives us.

Teacher: How are you, Sprout? Did you have something you forgot to tell us?

Sprout: I was thinking. . . . I don't always keep my promises or listen either.

Teacher: Does that get you into trouble?

Sprout: Sometimes. . . . My mom told me not to run on the broken sidewalk because I could fall. I really didn't think I would fall, so I didn't listen to her. But she was right. I fell and skinned my hand. It hurt!

Teacher: Was Mom angry that you didn't listen?

Sprout: Yes, and she was sad that I got hurt, but she forgave me. She told me God would forgive me for not listening too. He promises to forgive my sins because of Jesus. Even though my hand hurts, I know Jesus will make it well.

Teacher: God loves and forgives us. He keeps all His promises to us. Our God is so good! Sprout, would you like to sing a song with the boys and girls?

Sing "God Loves Me Dearly" (*LOSP*, p. 85; CD 10)

Craft Time

What you do: Give the children Craft Page 1, scissors, tape, and disposable cups to make story puppets. Before making the puppets, briefly review the story. Point to the Zechariah figure, or hold up the Zechariah puppet you made earlier.

Say **Pretend that you are Zechariah. Show how you would look if an angel came to see you. Can you make your face look afraid? How about surprised?**

When Zechariah came out to see the people, he couldn't talk. Pretend that you are Zechariah again. How will you tell the people that you saw an angel? How will you tell the people that you and Elizabeth are going to have a baby? Don't say a word; just show me.

God will keep His promise to Zechariah. How do you think Zechariah will feel when baby John is born? Yes, happy. Today, you will make storytelling puppets. You can use them to retell the story at home.

Growing in CHRIST.

Hand out the Craft Page and supplies. Have the children finish coloring the figures. Tell them to make the modern child look like them and to connect the dots to show a Bible story book. As you talk about how God keeps His promises to us, the children can draw a happy smile on the child's face.

Ask **Does God make promises to us too?** Accept answers. **God promises to make us His children in Baptism. He promises to forgive us and care for us. He promises to answer our prayers. Where do we find out about God's promises?** In the Bible! **We are happy that God keeps His promises to us. Draw a happy face on the child.**

Cut out the figures and tape the tabs together to make them stand up, or tape them around upside-down paper cups to make them into puppets.

Paper Plus option: Make angels using paper cups, Styrofoam balls or ribbon, chenille wires, and decorating supplies. Turn a paper cup upside down for the angel body. Glue on a small Styrofoam ball for the head, or cut a piece of ribbon and glue it around the middle of the cup to separate the head from the body. Have the children draw facial features on the head and decorate the angel with markers, glitter, rickrack, craft hair, and so forth. Cut triangle-shaped wings from paper or paper doilies, and tape to the body. Make a halo from a chenille wire.

Snack Time

What you do: Serve angel-shaped sugar cookies. Review the story as you enjoy the snack.

Live It Out

God gives us pastors and other church workers to teach us God's promises and tell us the Good News about Jesus. Use angel stamps or draw around angel-shaped cookie cutters to make thank-you cards to give to your pastor or deaconess or other church worker to say thank you for teaching us about Jesus. Provide decorating supplies to personalize the cards, and have children dictate what they want to say.

4 Closing (5 minutes)

Going Home

What you do: Gather the children's take-home things to send home with them. Give each child a 12-inch ribbon or a piece of crepe paper. Encourage the children to twirl the ribbons or wave the crepe paper as they sing.

Sing "God Has Sent His Angels Down" (*LOSP*, p. 26; CD 9) or "My Soul Rejoices" (*LSB* 933:1; CD 3)

Say **God promises to love and forgive you, and God always keeps His promises! Let's say "God keeps all His promises" together.** Do so.

Pray **Dear God, thank You for always keeping Your promises. Thank You for sending Jesus to be our Savior. Amen.**

Reflection

Which activities worked well today? Which ones didn't? Use this information to help you choose suitable activities for next week's lesson.

Special Delivery!

What do these people do for you?

Preparing the Lesson

The Birth of Jesus Foretold
Luke 1:26–38

Key Point

Because of Christ, God favored Mary and chose her to be the mother of the Savior. Because of Christ, God favors us and chooses us to be His children.

Law/**Gospel**

Like Mary, I deserve nothing from God because of my sinfulness. **God gives me unmerited grace and favor because of His Son.**

Context

The angel Gabriel visited both Zechariah, Elizabeth's husband, and Mary, Elizabeth's relative. Elizabeth was too old to have a baby, while Mary was too young—still a virgin—only engaged to be married.

Commentary

This story about Mary begins "in the sixth month" (v. 26), that is, six months after John the Baptist was conceived. Gabriel appears to Mary with a message from God: " The Holy Spirit will come upon you, and the power of the Most High will overshadow you" (v. 35). This came about exactly as Gabriel described it would: the Holy Spirit conceived Jesus Christ within Mary.

While Elizabeth had the support of her husband, Mary faced the possible loss of her reputation, her family, her fiancé, and even her life. Not only could she be stoned to death for supposed adultery, but she could also die because of complications of pregnancy and childbirth. In spite of the looming mix of joy and fear at Gabriel's message, Mary did not question God. She submitted to His will because she first received the Gospel, the Christ to be born from her womb. Her faith accepted the unacceptable, and for Christ's sake, all generations do call her blessed.

As Paul says in Philippians 1:6, any good work or blessing comes through Jesus Christ alone, who will complete that good work in the day of His second coming, even as He will execute judgment on the wicked.

The Good News of Christ embraces both His suffering and death for us on Calvary and also His return as Lord and Judge. It is His Word that counts, not the words of the world. That means we can trust His Word in spite of all worldly cares and fears. We can accept the unacceptable in Christ's name.

Like Mary, we can bear the most fearful of crosses that God gives us as blessings in Christ. We believe that the worst evil that might strike us in this world cannot overcome the Judge of all worlds and ages. Our victory in Christ is an eternal victory. Like Mary, we are eternally blessed.

To hear an in-depth discussion of this Bible account, visit cph.org/podcast and listen to our Seeds of Faith podcast each week.

Preparing the Lesson © 2006, 2015 Concordia Publishing House. Scripture: ESV®.

The Birth of Jesus Foretold

Luke 1:26–38

Connections

Bible Words
The Lord has chosen you.
Deuteronomy 14:2

Faith Word
Good News

Hymn
My Soul Rejoices
(*LSB* 933; CD 3)

Catechism
Apostles' Creed: Second Article

Take-Home Point
God chose me to be His child.

① Opening (15 minutes)

Welcome Time

What you do: Set up two activity areas to build interest. In one, set out copies of Activity Page 2A, markers, crayons, and decorating supplies such as rickrack and glitter pens. Make copies of Activity Page Fun (below and on CD) for parents or a classroom helper. Adjust talk as necessary.

In the other activity area, set out play dough and cookie cutters in the shape of an angel or circle and triangle. To make your own salt play dough, mix 2 cups of flour, 1 cup of salt, and 1 cup of water. Add additional water or oil if dough is crumbly.

Play the CD from your Teacher Tools. Greet the children, give them a sticker to put on the attendance chart, and have them put their offering in the basket.

Say Hi, [Adrian]. How are you? I wonder . . . do you choose what you want to play with or have for breakfast? Today, you'll hear how God chose Mary to do something special.

Activity Page Fun Get a copy of Activity Page 2A and decorating supplies. Show the page to your child.

Ask What is this a picture of? An angel. **Where do you think angels live? What do they do?** Give your child crayons and other supplies to decorate the angel. **In the Bible story today, you'll hear about an angel who brought good news to a woman named Mary. Be sure to listen to find out what he told her.**

© 2015 Concordia Publishing House. Reproduced by permission. Available on the Teacher CD.

MATERIALS NEEDED

1 Opening	2 God Speaks	3 We Live	4 Closing
Teacher Tools Attendance chart & CD	**Teacher Tools** Storytelling Figures 2-1 to 2-3 Background A & CD	**Student Pack** Craft Page 2 Sticker	**Teacher Tools** CD
Student Pack Attendance sticker	**Student Pack** Lesson Leaflet 2 & stickers	**Other Supplies** Bookmark or other gift Sprout or another puppet Sugar cookies & tube frosting Paper Plus supplies (optional)	**Student Pack** Take-home materials
Other Supplies Activity Page 2A (TG) Play dough & cookie cutters Decorating supplies (optional) Pictures of angels (optional) Resource Page 1 (TG)	**Other Supplies** Envelope & letter Baby picture *Mary's Christmas Story* Arch Book (optional) Jesus picture, garland & towel (optional)		

Active Learning Encourage children to cut out angels. If you provided circle and triangle cookie cutters, show students how the triangle can be used to make an angel body and the circle can be used to make a head. The children can cut out their own angels after they have had some time to manipulate the clay. The play dough can be used again if stored in an airtight container, or the angels can be left out to dry. Next week, let the children paint them and take them home.

Option: Set out pictures or create a PowerPoint slide show of angels shown in classical art, or if your church has stained glass windows depicting angels, take pictures of them on your tablet device to show the children.

Use your classroom signal to let the children know it's time to clean up and gather for circle time. Sing a cleanup song (Resource Page 1).

Say When you are done cleaning up, pretend you are angel, and come sit by me.

Gathering in God's Name

What you do: Gather the children, and begin with this opening. To teach about the Church Year, use the materials in the Church Year Worship Kit (see the introduction for more information).

Sing "Our Church Family" (*LOSP*, p. 11; CD 15) or another opening song

Say God loves you very much! You and I are part of God's Church family because God chose us through Baptism and His Word to be His children!

Invite the children to say the Invocation and Amen with you. Tell them "Amen" is the special word they get to say at the end of prayers, hymns, and parts of the church service.

Begin In the name of the Father and of the Son and of the Holy Spirit. Amen.

Offering Have a child bring the offering basket forward. Sing an offering song.

Pray Dear Father in heaven, thank You for loving us and sending Jesus to be our Savior. Thank You for choosing us to be Your children. Help us to listen. Help us to learn more about Your love. In Jesus' name we pray. Amen.

Celebrate Birthdays, Baptism birthdays, and special occasions

② God Speaks (20 minutes)

Story Clue

What you do: Before class, write the words *Good News* on a piece of paper. Add a picture of a baby or something that implies it is about a baby. Place the paper in a large envelope, and put your name on it. If possible, have someone deliver the envelope to you. If not, pick it up and appear surprised. Express curiosity about its contents. Allow children to speculate on its contents too.

Say I wonder what is in this envelope. It looks like it is important. Maybe

it's a letter. Hmm, I wonder who sent it to me? Should I open it?

Open the envelope and remove the letter. Show surprise at its contents. Tell the children that the letter is telling you about someone who is going to have a baby. Turn the paper for the children to see, and point out the picture of the baby.

Say **This paper has good news. It says a friend of mine is going to have a baby. I'm so excited! It is good news when a baby is going to be born.**

This letter reminds me of what the Bible tells us about a woman named Mary, who got good news in a special way. And it wasn't just good news for Mary. It was good news for us too! Let's listen, and I will tell you this true story from God's Word, the Bible. Open Bible.

Bible Story Time

What you do: Use Background A and the storytelling figures to teach the Bible story. Use a restickable glue stick (see Introduction for more information), double-stick tape, or loops of tape to attach the figures to the background.

Use the following script, pointing to the angel and Mary figures as indicated. Place the figures in your Bible. To get the children's attention, hold up your hand or a picture of Jesus. Have your CD cued up to track 13, ready to play "Jesus, Our Good Friend" at the end of the story.

Option: Ask two children to pretend to be the angel and Mary. Put garland on the head of the child who is the angel. Give the child acting as Mary a towel for a head covering. Stand behind the character who is talking as you speak the dialogue. Directions are given in the script for this option too. You can also tell the story using the Arch Book *Mary's Christmas Story* (CPH, 59-1499).

Say **I need to see everyone's eyes here** (hold up hand or picture of Jesus), **so I know you are ready to listen to our story from God's Word.** Open your Bible.

The Bible tells us about a young woman named Mary. Add Mary (2-1) to the background or point to child playing Mary. **Mary was going to be married to a man named Joseph.** Add table (2-2) to Background A. **One day, God sent an angel to tell her something important.** Add angel (2-3) or point to angel. **Mary was surprised and afraid when she saw the angel. Let's listen to what they said.**

Angel: (*Point to angel, or stand behind child playing the angel.*) Hello, Mary. My name is Gabriel. God has sent me to tell you that He has a special plan for you.

Mary: (*Point to Mary, or stand behind child playing Mary.*) Oh, you frightened me! I've never seen an angel before.

Angel: You don't need to be afraid, Mary. God is with you. He has sent me to give you good news. He has chosen you to be the mother of His Son! Yes, that's right. You are going to have a baby! And this baby will be the most special baby in the whole world. He will be our Savior, Jesus. God is sending Him to save all people from sin so they can go to heaven someday.

Mary: (*Puzzled*) I don't understand. How can this happen? I am not married yet.

Gabriel: God can do all things. Your cousin Elizabeth is very old, but she is going to have a baby too. God made it possible for her to have a baby. He will make it possible for you.

Key Point

Because of Christ, God favored Mary and chose her to be the mother of the Savior. Because of Christ, God favors us and chooses us to be His children.

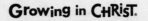

Mary: (*Excited and happy*) Even though this is hard to understand, I trust God because I know He loves me. I am His servant. I am happy to do what He wants.

Say Mary was surprised to see the angel that day. But she was happy when she heard the angel's good news. God was keeping the promise He had made long ago. He was sending His Son, Jesus, to be the Savior. And God had chosen Mary to be His mother!

Sing "Jesus, Our Good Friend" (*LOSP*, p. 77; CD 13)

Bible Story Review

What you do: Hand out Lesson Leaflet 2, stickers, and crayons. Point to the leaflet picture and use the questions to review the story. Do the leaflet activities; then lead the children in the action poem.

Ask **Who came to see Mary?** The angel Gabriel

What good news did the angel tell Mary? She would have a baby.

Who will Mary's baby be? Our Savior, Jesus

Point to the picture on the front of the leaflet, and have the children identify the two characters. Have them use their finger to connect the angel and Mary in the sidebar to the angel and Mary in the big picture. Give them stickers to add to the leaflet page. Do the dot-to-dot activity on the front and then the back of the leaflet.

Ask **Where does God tell us the good news about Jesus?** (In the Bible) Turn the page. **The Bible tells us that God sent an angel to tell Mary good news.**

Ask **What did he tell her?** (Mary would be the mother of God's Son.)

Say **Now, I want you to stand up. When you hear me say "Good News," say those words after me and clap two times.** Demonstrate.

Great Idea!

God sent an angel to Mary.
Good news! Good news! *Clap. Clap.*
The angel told Mary, "You will have a baby."
Good news! Good news! *Clap. Clap.*
The baby will be Jesus, God's Son.
Good news! Good news! *Clap. Clap.*
God loves us and sent Jesus to save us.
Good news! Good news! *Clap. Clap.*

Bible Words

What you do: Mark Deuteronomy 14:2 in your Bible. Lead the children in the action poem; then open your Bible and read the Bible Words.

Say **I open my Bible book up wide**
Hold your hands, palms together, in front of you.
And read the words that are inside.
Open your hands, keeping them together as an open book.
The Bible tells us, "The Lᴏʀᴅ has chosen you."

Ask **Do you think God chose Mary to be Jesus' mother because she never did anything bad?** Let children answer.

Say   No, Mary said and did bad things too! She was a sinner like us. Even though she didn't deserve it, God loved her, and Mary believed in Him. Out of love, God chose her to be Jesus' mother.

Even though we don't deserve it, God chooses us, too, in a different way, to be His children! He does this through Baptism and His Word. In Baptism, God washes away our sins because of Jesus and gives us faith to believe in Him. In His Word, the Bible, God tells us the Good News about Jesus, who came to be our Savior from sin.

Let's say our Bible Words again. Repeat action rhyme and say Bible Words.

3 We Live (15 minutes)

Use these activities to help the children grow in their understanding of what the Bible story means for their lives. Choose the ones that work best with your class.

Growing through God's Word

What you do: Bring out Sprout and a small gift, such as a bookmark.

Teacher: Hello, Sprout! It looks like you have something special. What is it?

Sprout: I have something for you. It's a gift!

Teacher: How nice! But why did you choose me for a gift? Did I do something special? Did I help you, or—?

Sprout: (*Interrupts*) No, no. You didn't do anything. I chose you just because I love you. That's why I want to give you this gift!

Teacher: (*Taking gift and looking at it*) This is a nice gift. Thank you, Sprout! But thank you most of all for loving me!

Say   Boys and girls, this reminds me of how God loves us and wants us to be His children. Remember, He didn't choose us to be His children because we're strong or pretty or run fast or sing great or try to be good. No, He chose us because He loves us. And that's why He made a plan to send Jesus to be born of Mary.

We all think and say and do bad things. We sin. But God sent Jesus to pay for our sins on the cross. Because of Jesus, God forgives our sins. Because of Jesus, He makes us His children by washing away our sins in Baptism.

I am happy God chose me to be His child! Smile. **If you are happy God chose you to be His child, show me your happy face.** Smile.

Craft Time

What you do: Give children Craft Page 2, a baby Jesus sticker, and crayons. Point to the angel on the Craft Page.

Say   **Today, you will make a door hanger.** Point to side 1. **The words say, "Someone's coming, someone special: Jesus, our good friend."** Read the Bible Words. **God sent an angel to tell Mary that God chose her to be the mother of His Son.**

Growing in CHRIST

Turn to side 2. Read the Bible Words and the song refrain at the top.

Say **Jesus was born at Christmas to be our Savior!**

Give children a Jesus sticker to add to the manger. Have them cut along the cut line and cut out the middle of their hanger. Give help, as needed.

Paper Plus option: Make copies of Activity Page 2B for each child. Have children color the figures of the angel and Mary; then follow the directions to make story puppets or a Bible scroll of the story.

Snack Time

What you do: Provide round sugar cookies and tubes of yellow, black, and red frosting. Have children decorate the cookies to look like angel faces (e.g., black dots for eyes, a red smile, and a yellow halo at top).

Live It Out

Ask **Do you remember what Mary said to Gabriel when he told her God had chosen her to be Jesus' mother? She said, "Behold, I am a servant of the Lord. I believe your words." God has chosen us too. We are His children. By His power, we, too, can say, "I am Your servant. I believe what You say in Your Word."**

What can you do this week as God's child to serve others?

Help the children think of ways they can show God's love for others in response to His love for us in Jesus. Make a class list of ideas. Challenge children to choose one thing on the list to do this week.

 **4 Closing** (5 minutes)

Going Home

What you do: Gather the children's take-home things to send home with them.

Sing "God Has Sent His Angels Down" (*LOSP*, p. 26; CD 9) or "My Soul Rejoices" (*LSB* 933:1; CD 3)

Say **God sent an angel to Mary. The angel told her that God chose her to be the mother of His Son, Jesus. That is good news! God chose us to be His children. That's good news too! Let's say "God chose me to be His child" together.** Do so.

Pray **Thank You, God, for sending baby Jesus to be our Savior. Thank You for forgiving our sins and choosing us to be Your children. In Jesus' name we pray. Amen.**

Reflection

Did you smile with joy when you talked about the Good News of God's great love for us in Jesus? Who else smiled? Joy is contagious. Share God's love in a joyful way with the children you teach!

Directions: Cut out the figures. Make story puppets by taping the bottom strips into circles so the figures will be freestanding, or attach the figures to upside down cups.

To make a Bible scroll of the story, cut out the figures without the base strips, and attach them to legal-size paper or a piece of brown paper bag or parcel paper. Roll each end of the paper around a wooden dowel and glue or tape in place. See illustration.

Roll the dowel ends toward the center until they meet. Tie with a piece of ribbon. Unroll the scroll to "read" the story.

↑
Cut apart.

25

Preparing the Lesson

Mary Visits Elizabeth

Luke 1:39–56

Key Point

God remembered Mary, filling her womb with the world's Savior. God remembers us and, through His Word and Sacraments, fills us with Christ Jesus, granting us full salvation. Like Mary, we offer our humble praise.

Law/Gospel

No one is righteous before God. **God sent His Son, Jesus, the Righteous One, to be born of Mary, so He could give me His righteousness, granting me full salvation.**

Context

Luke 1:26–38 records the announcement of Jesus' birth to Mary in Nazareth by the angel Gabriel, who came to Mary in the sixth month of Elizabeth's pregnancy and announced the birth of Jesus.

Verses 39–45 tell of Mary's visit with Elizabeth in the hill country of Judea. Mary's arrival at her relative's house evoked the response of Elizabeth that proclaimed the blessedness of Mary and of the fruit of her womb.

Finally, verses 46–56 record the Magnificat (Mary's hymn of praise), where Mary "magnified" God for the rich blessings He had bestowed on her, His lowly servant.

Commentary

After the angel Gabriel's announcement to Mary that she would be the mother of the Son of God, Mary hurried to see her relative Elizabeth. When Mary came in contact with Elizabeth, the presence of God caused John to leap in his mother's womb. With God in her presence and a babe who had just leapt, Elizabeth broke forth in a worshiplike response and proclaimed the blessedness of Mary, but even more, the blessedness of what was contained in Mary's womb.

Jesus Christ is that blessed fruit of Mary's womb (v. 42), and where He comes bodily, it is always a cosmic event, conveying grace and love. Even today, when Christ comes with His body and blood to our altars, a cosmic event occurs as the burden of sin is removed and we are joined to Him.

Following Elizabeth's response, Mary sang her own hymn of praise (the Magnificat). In this hymn, Mary set forth one of the central themes in God's plan of salvation: the great reversal.

This God who became a man, this shepherd who became a lamb, this priest who became a sacrifice, this host who became a meal did so that those humbled and hungry from the burden and barrenness of sin might be exalted and filled with good things. Mary was, and so are we. God has remembered us (v. 54) and filled us with the greatest of all things, His own Son, Jesus Christ.

To hear an in-depth discussion of this Bible account, visit cph.org/podcast and listen to our Seeds of Faith podcast each week.

Lesson 3
Mary Visits Elizabeth
Luke 1:39–56

Connections

Bible Words
My spirit rejoices in God my Savior. Luke 1:47

Faith Word
Joy

Hymn
My Soul Rejoices
(*LSB* 933; CD 3)

Catechism
Apostles' Creed: Second Article

Liturgy
Magnificat

Take-Home Point
God gives me joy in Jesus.

1 Opening (15 minutes)

Welcome Time

What you do: Set up two activity areas to build interest and readiness for the lesson. In one, set out copies of Activity Page 3 and crayons. Make copies of Activity Page Fun (below and on CD) for parents or a classroom helper. Adjust talk as necessary.

In the other activity area, set out precut squares of wrapping paper, gift bags, bows, tape, and empty boxes or blocks for the children to wrap.

Play the CD from your Teacher Tools. Greet the children, give them a sticker to put on the attendance chart, and have them put their offering in the basket.

Say   Hi, [Aubrey]. It's good to see you here! I wonder . . . do you like to get gifts? Today we're going to talk about the best gift of all.

Activity Page Fun Get a copy of Activity Page 3. Show the page to your child. Talk about giving gifts.

Ask   What do you see on this page? Yes, there is a big gift box and lots of presents around it. Point to something you'd like to get as a gift.

Do you like to give gifts to others? Who is someone you would like to give a gift to? Let your child name someone. **Circle something that you would like to give [name of person].**

We give gifts to show people that we love them. Receiving a gift often makes us feel happy. God gives us many good gifts. Today, you will hear about gifts God gives us out of His love for us, especially one very special gift. Listen and find out what it is.

MATERIALS NEEDED

1 Opening	2 God Speaks	3 We Live	4 Closing
Teacher Tools Attendance chart & CD	**Teacher Tools** Poster B	**Teacher Tools** CD	**Teacher Tools** CD
Student Pack Attendance sticker	**Student Pack** Lesson Leaflet 3 Stickers	**Student Pack** Craft Page 3 Stickers	**Student Pack** Take-home items
Other Supplies Activity Page 3 Wrapping-paper, bows, gift bags & ribbon Blocks or boxes Resource Page 1 (TG)	**Other Supplies** Sprout or another puppet	**Other Supplies** Rhythm instruments or homemade bells Hole punch, yarn, or ribbon Bugle-shaped snack chips Decorating supplies (optional) Paper Plus supplies (optional)	

Active Learning Set out precut squares of wrapping paper, gift bags, bows, tape, and empty boxes or blocks for the children to wrap. Encourage the children to wrap the boxes or blocks and pretend they are gifts. Discuss gift giving as they do this.

Say At Christmas or when someone is having a birthday, we might give that person a gift. We wrap our gifts in pretty paper or put them in gift bags, just as you are doing today. We give people presents to show them we love them. Today, you will hear about a special gift God promised to give us because He loves us.

Use your classroom signal to let the children know it's time to clean up and gather for circle time. Sing a cleanup song (Resource Page 1).

Say Pretend it is your birthday and it's time to open gifts as you come to our story area today.

Gathering in God's Name

What you do: Gather the children, and begin with this opening. To teach about the Church Year, use the materials in the Church Year Worship Kit (see the introduction for more information).

Sing "Our Church Family" (*LOSP*, p. 11; CD 15) or another opening song

Say God loves you very much! You and I are part of God's Church family because God chose us through Baptism and His Word to be His children!

Invite the children to say the Invocation and Amen with you. Tell them "Amen" is the special word they get to say at the end of prayers, hymns, and parts of the church service.

Begin In the name of the Father and of the Son and of the Holy Spirit. Amen.

Offering Have a child bring the offering basket forward. Sing an offering song.

Pray Dear Father in heaven, thank You for loving us and giving us good gifts, especially, Jesus, our Savior. Help us to learn more about Your love. In Jesus' name we pray. Amen.

Celebrate Birthdays, Baptism birthdays, and special occasions

2 God Speaks (20 minutes)

Story Clue

What you do: Use Sprout or another puppet to set the stage for the story.

Sprout: (*Humming "Hark the Herald Angels Sing"*) Hi, Teacher! Hi, kids!

Teacher: Hi, Sprout. You sound happy.

Sprout: Yes, I am full of joy! We had a hymn sing before church, and the pastor let me pick!

Teacher: How special! Which hymn did you choose?

Sprout: One of my favorites all year round! I love it because it tells about Jesus' birth. You know (*starting to sing*), "Hark! The hairy old angels sing, glory to the newborn king."

Teacher: (*Smiling*) That is one of my favorites too, Sprout. But it isn't about "hairy old" angels; it's about "herald" angels. *Herald* means the angels came to tell everyone important news from God. Herald angels are God's messengers.

Sprout: Oh, that makes more sense! The angels are telling about Jesus' birth, aren't they? That's why I love that hymn!

Teacher: You are right, Sprout. But even before Jesus was born, God sent the angel Gabriel to get people ready for Jesus' birth. First, He sent His angel to Zechariah with the news that baby John would be born. Then He sent the angel Gabriel with important news for Mary. (*Whisper:*) She was going to have a baby too! Let's find out more about that special time. (*Put Sprout where he can "listen."*)

Bible Story Time

What you do: You will need Poster B from your Teacher Tools.

Say The hymn Sprout picked for the hymn sing today is one we sing at Christmas. **What other things do you do at Christmas?** Accept responses. **I like to open gifts and watch others open the gifts I gave them. We give gifts at Christmas and birthdays and other special times to show love for others. It makes me happy to give and receive gifts and to show love and know that I am loved.**

Open Bible. **The Bible tells us that God loves us so much that He wanted to give the world a special gift too. His people had been waiting and waiting for the promised Savior. When the time was right for Jesus to be born, God sent an angel to Mary.**

The angel told Mary, "I have good news for you. Soon, you will have a baby. This baby is special. He is God's Son. God wants you to name Him Jesus because He will save people from their sins."

"How can this be?" Mary asked. "I am not married yet."

"God will make this happen," said the angel. "He can do anything! Your relative Elizabeth is also going to have a baby, even though she is very old."

Mary knew God would do what He promised. Mary said, "I am God's servant. I will do whatever God asks me to do."

After that, Mary hurried to see Elizabeth. When Mary went into the house, the baby inside of Elizabeth jumped for joy. Show Poster B. **Mary told Elizabeth about the angel's visit. Elizabeth told Mary she was blessed because she would be the mother of God's Son!**

Then Mary sang a song to praise God. Sometimes, we sing Mary's song in church. It is called the Magnificat. That's a big word, isn't it? Let's say it together. Say *Magnificat* with the children. **Mary rejoiced that she would be Jesus' mother. Elizabeth rejoiced when she saw Mary. The baby inside Elizabeth leaped for joy. We rejoice that Jesus was born for us too. Jesus gives us joy because He saves us from our sins.**

Key Point

God remembered Mary, filling her womb with the world's Savior. God remembers us and, through His Word and Sacraments, fills us with Christ Jesus, granting us full salvation. Like Mary, we offer our humble praise.

Bible Story Review

What you do: Hand out Lesson Leaflet 3, crayons, and a sticker of Jesus. Review the story using the questions or the game. Then look at the leaflet together.

Ask **Who are the people in the picture?** Mary and Elizabeth

What happy news does Mary have? She is going to have a baby.

What happy news does God give us? The baby Mary will have is God's Son, Jesus. He is the Savior God promised to send.

Option: Play a version of Mother May I? For each yes question, have the children jump forward one jump. For each no, the children must jump backward one jump. Use questions like the following.

Did Mary see an angel? Yes

Did the angel bring a pizza? No

Did the angel say that Mary would have a baby boy? Yes

Did Mary visit a police officer? No

Did Mary visit Elizabeth? Yes

Did Mary sing a special song to praise God? Yes

Can we praise God? Yes

Point to the sidebar activity on side 1 of the leaflet. Have the children identify and color the women and then color the gift and add a sticker of baby Jesus to it. Talk about how Jesus is God's gift to us. Because Jesus paid for our sins on the cross, God forgives us and gives us eternal life with Him.

On side 2, talk about how having Jesus as our Savior gives us a special kind of happiness called "joy" as students color the picture. Children process and retain information better when they use their large muscles. If you did not play the game, do the action poem on side 2 of the leaflet.

Bible Words

What you do: Read the Bible Words from Luke 1:47 in your Bible so the children know it is God's Word.

Say **"My spirit rejoices in God my Savior." These are the words that Mary said in her song. She rejoiced that God was keeping His promise to send Jesus to be our Savior. She rejoiced that she would be His mother.**

Jesus is your Savior too. You, too, can say, "My spirit rejoices in God my Savior." Let's say those words together now. Do so.

Elizabeth's baby leaped for joy inside Elizabeth. We can too. Let's jump for joy as we say our Bible Words.

Say **My spirit** *Jump.*
rejoices *Jump.*
in God *Jump.*
my Savior. *Jump.*

3 We Live (15 minutes)

Use these activities to help the children grow in their understanding of what the Bible story means for their lives. Choose the ones that work best with your class.

Growing through God's Word

What you do: Thread jingle bells onto ribbon or chenille wires. If you don't have instruments, have children clap their hands. Have your CD ready to play.

Say **God loved Mary. He gave her a special gift. She would be Jesus' mother. That news filled Mary with a special kind of happiness called joy. Joy is something God gives. It comes from knowing that Jesus is our Savior.**

Jesus is God's gift to us too. He came to be our Savior. He saves us from being punished for all the wrong things we think and say and do—the things we call sins. When we do something wrong, we can tell God we're sorry. God will forgive us for Jesus' sake.

Mary sang a song to praise God for His love. When I hear that God loves me and sent Jesus to be my Savior, I want to sing for joy too. Let's sing together to show our joy that Jesus is our Savior.

Sing "I Have the Joy" (*LOSP*, p. 62) or "Praise Him, Praise Him" (*LOSP*, p. 68)

Say **Now let's shake our bells/musical instruments to praise God.**

Play "My Soul Rejoices," which is a hymn version of the Magnificat (CD 3). Give the children jingle bells or rhythm instruments to play as you lead them around the room.

Craft Time

What you do: Use Craft Page 3, stickers, crayons, yarn, and a hole punch to make two ornaments that the children can hang up at home. Talk about the ornament with the angel first. *Option:* Supply glitter glue, sequins, bits of ribbon, and raffia to decorate the ornaments. Protect the work area with newspaper.

Ask **Who is this?** (The angel Gabriel!) **What good news does the angel tell Mary?** (Jesus is coming!)

Have the children color the border around the angel and add stickers to it. They can color the straw in the manger on the other side or glue pieces of yellow paper or raffia to it. Then direct their attention to the second ornament.

Say **Here is Mary. God sent the angel to tell Mary she would be Jesus' mother.** Turn the ornament over. Give each child a sticker of baby Jesus to put in Mary's arms. **God gives good gifts! Jesus is our best gift. He came to be our Savior. Because of Jesus, God gives us many other good gifts too. He forgives our sins and gives us a home in heaven with Him. Knowing Jesus is our Savior gives us joy.**

Ask **What are some other gifts God gives us?** Talk about some of these with the children as they color and add stickers to this ornament.

Then punch a hole at the top of each ornament, and string it with yarn or ribbon for easy hanging at home, or send the page home intact for the children to cut out and finish there.

Paper Plus option: Make bells. Provide Styrofoam cups, jingle bells, yarn or chenille wires, and decorating materials for the children to personalize their bells (e.g., markers, rickrack, ribbon, stickers or stamps, or glitter).

Thread a jingle bell onto a piece of yarn, or twist it onto a piece of chenille wire. Poke holes in the top of the cup and tie the yarn, or poke the chenille wire through it so that the jingle bell hangs inside the cup like a ringer.

Snack Time

What you do: Serve bugle-shaped snack chips. Talk about how the shape reminds us of trumpets, which people play to make a joyful noise to the Lord.

Live It Out

Video-record the children singing "I Have the Joy" or "Praise Him, Praise Him." Give them jingle bells to shake or rhythm instruments to play as they sing. Ask your pastor to share the video with homebound or elderly members. *Option:* Arrange a field trip to a local care facility where children can sing Jesus songs to share their joy in Jesus with residents.

 **4 Closing** (5 minutes)

Going Home

What you do: Gather the children's take-home things to send home with them.

Sing "God Loves Me Dearly" (*LOSP*, p. 85; CD 10) or "My Soul Rejoices" (*LSB* 933:1; CD 3)

Say **God sent Jesus to be our Savior. Knowing that Jesus is my Savior gives me joy. God forgives our sins for Jesus' sake and gives us life with Him forever. Knowing that I am forgiven through Jesus gives me joy.**

Let's say "God gives me joy in Jesus" together. Do so.

Pray **Dear God,* thank You for sending baby Jesus to be our Savior.* Thank You for loving us* and giving us every good gift.* Amen.*** *Have children echo words at asterisk.

Reflection

Adding movement and actions can reinforce learning. Did the children enjoy jumping for joy when they said their Bible Words? Did they like shaking bells or playing instruments? Evaluate how these activities worked. If they seemed to help the children learn the material better, consider how you can incorporate more movement activities into other lessons.

Which gift would you give to your friend?

Preparing the Lesson

_____

The Birth of John

Luke 1:57–80

Key Point

Through Zechariah, God said John would give knowledge of salvation to His people in the forgiveness of sins. Through His Holy Word, God speaks to give us knowledge of salvation and forgiveness through His Son, Jesus.

Law/**Gospel**

As a child of the first parents, Adam and Eve, I am sinful and in need of salvation. **John, the son of Elizabeth and Zechariah, and others who proclaim the Good News point me to Jesus, the Lamb of God, who takes away the sin of the world.**

Context

With friends and relatives gathered on the eighth day after the birth of his son, Zechariah proclaims the boy's name is John. His startling announcement and restored voice allow Zechariah to prophesy concerning his son's future ministry.

Commentary

Elizabeth and Zechariah, both of pure Levite ancestry, were pious and observant of the Torah, the instruction concerning the commands and blessings of the Lord. Their son was born the greatest of all earthly Levites, surpassing even Aaron and second only to his relative Jesus, although the Christian priesthood shared by all believers would be greater still (Matthew 11:11–15). Zechariah's relatives had their own plans, which were different from God's. So Zechariah faced a "fork in the road." Being devoted to God's Word, as was his wife, he followed that Word and fulfilled the prophecy by naming his son John. As a result, God lifted the cross of muteness, and Zechariah prophesied concerning his son and the Christ who would follow.

We have no alternative but to go back to the basics—to our baptismal identity and the Word of God—if we are to keep walking in God's light even when faced with a serious "fork in the road."

God's Word comforts us when we go to it as the wellspring of faith. God's Word strengthens us when we falter. As with Zechariah, it guides us when a turning point to or away from God is at hand. As with Zechariah, it gives us the hindsight to see our past trials as true blessings that have built us up in faith.

The Lord is near; rejoice! You, who have been made to walk in His light, praise Him! Your deliverance is at hand!

To hear an in-depth discussion of this Bible account, visit cph.org/podcast and listen to our Seeds of Faith podcast each week.

Preparing the Lesson © 2006, 2015 Concordia Publishing House. Scripture: ESV®.

Lesson 4
The Birth of John
Luke 1:57–80

Connections

Bible Words
With God all things are possible. Matthew 19:26

Faith Word
Prepare

Hymn
O Jesus So Sweet, O Jesus So Mild (*LSB* 546; CD 4)

Catechism
Apostles' Creed: Second Article

Liturgy
Benedictus

Take-Home Point
God's Word tells me about Jesus.

1 Opening (15 minutes)

Welcome Time

What you do: Set up two activity areas to build interest and readiness for the lesson. In one, set out copies of Activity Page 4 and crayons. Make copies of Activity Page Fun (below and on CD) for parents or a classroom helper. Adjust talk as necessary.

In the other activity area, set out dolls and baby items (e.g., rattles, clothes, bottles), or make arrangements to take the children on a field trip to your church sanctuary.

Play the CD from your Teacher Tools. Greet the children, give them a sticker to put on the attendance chart, and have them put their offering in the basket.

Say Hi, [Henry]. Have you been to church yet? What did Pastor do? Pastors help us learn about Jesus, don't they?

Activity Page Fun Get a copy of Activity Page 4. Show it to your child.

Ask Who is this a picture of? (A pastor) I wonder . . . what do pastors do? Let child share thoughts. **This pastor is in church. What is the book beside him? Pastors tell us what God's Word says about Jesus, don't they? Draw a line from the Bible to the pastor's hand.**

In our Bible story today, you will hear about someone God sent to help people get ready for Jesus. Listen to find out his name.

Encourage your child to trace the dot-to-dot cross and color the page.

© 2015 Concordia Publishing House. Reproduced by permission. Available on the Teacher CD.

MATERIALS NEEDED

1 Opening	2 God Speaks	3 We Live	4 Closing
Teacher Tools Attendance chart & CD	**Teacher Tools** Storytelling Figures 4-1 to 4-5 Background A Poster A	**Teacher Tools** CD	**Teacher Tools** CD
Student Pack Attendance sticker	**Student Pack** Lesson Leaflet 4	**Student Pack** Craft Page 4 Stickers	**Student Pack** Take-home items
Other Supplies Activity Page 4 (TG) Dolls & baby items Resource Page 1 (TG)	**Other Supplies** Story bag & Christmas items *His Name Is John!* Arch Book (optional)	**Other Supplies** Story bag with church directory, Bible, shell & Communion wafers Graham crackers, frosting or cream cheese & plastic knives Paper Plus supplies (optional)	

Active Learning Let the children take care of the babies. Tell them that they will hear about the birth of a special baby today.

Option: Take the children on a field trip to your church sanctuary, or use your tablet device to take pictures of the things we see in church (altar, pulpit, font, etc.). Ask children what happens at the baptismal font, the altar, the pulpit, and so forth. Show them the Bible on the pulpit or lectern and ask whom we hear about in the Bible. Point out the paraments and banners.

Great Idea!

Use your classroom signal to let the children know it's time to clean up and gather for circle time. Sing a cleanup song (Resource Page 1).

Say Shh. Today's story is about a baby. Let's pretend he is sleeping in our room. Walk as quietly as you can to our story area today.

Gathering in God's Name

What you do: Gather the children, and begin with this opening. To teach about the Church Year, use the materials in the Church Year Worship Kit (see the introduction for more information).

15

Sing "Our Church Family" (*LOSP*, p. 11; CD 15) or another opening song

Say You and I are part of God's church family. At church, the pastor teaches us about Jesus from God's Word. He tells us God forgives us for Jesus' sake. We get to sing and pray and give thanks. Today, we'll learn about a man God sent to help people get ready for Jesus.

Invite the children to say the Invocation and Amen with you. Tell them "Amen" is the special word they get to say at the end of prayers, hymns, and parts of the church service.

Begin In the name of the Father and of the Son and of the Holy Spirit. Amen.

Offering Have a child bring the offering basket forward. Sing an offering song.

Pray Dear Father, thank You for the Bible, where we learn about You and Your love for us. Thank You for sending Jesus to be our Savior. In His name we pray. Amen.

Celebrate Birthdays, Baptism birthdays, and special occasions

2 God Speaks (20 minutes)

Story Clue

What you do: In a story bag, put items that help us get ready for Christmas (e.g., a jingle bell, a scented candle, nativity figures, and garland). *Option:* Use items for a different church celebration, such as Easter, and adjust talk.

Say Let's play a guessing game about getting ready. Here is how we play: I will give you some clues, and you guess what I am getting ready for. Are you ready? Here is the first set of clues.

I put on my pajamas. I brush my teeth. I find a storybook to read. I say my prayers. I turn off the light. What am I getting ready for? (Going to sleep)

I put on my bathing suit. **Someone puts sunscreen on me. I gather my bucket and sand toys. What am I getting ready for?** (Going to the beach)

For our last set of clues, I put some things in my story bag that help us get ready for a special time in church. Let's see if you can guess what I am getting ready for.

Take the items out of your bag one at a time. As you say what the item is, let the children smell or touch or listen to it.

Say **I light a candle. I jingle the bells. I hang the garland. I put up a nativity set. What do these things help me get ready for? Christmas! Long ago, on that first Christmas, God sent Jesus to be born as our Savior.**

Today, I am going to tell you a true story from the Bible about another special baby. When this baby grew up, God used him to get people ready for Jesus, our Savior.

Bible Story Time

What you do: Use Background A and the storytelling figures to teach the Bible story. Place the figures in your Bible. Use a restickable glue stick, double-stick tape, or loops of tape to attach the figures when you tell the story. You will also need Poster A. *Option:* Use the Arch Book *His Name Is John!* (CPH, 59-2207) to tell or review the story.

Say **Today's story from the Bible is about Zechariah and Elizabeth and the baby God promised to give them.** Open your Bible and briefly hold up storytelling figures of Zechariah (4-1) and Elizabeth (4-2). **Do you remember how Zechariah was working in the temple one day when an angel came and stood by him?** Show Poster A. **The angel told Zechariah some happy news. He said that Zechariah and Elizabeth would have a baby.**

Zechariah thought they were too old to have a baby. Zechariah did not remember what God's Word tells us: "With God all things are possible." He had a hard time believing what the angel told him. So, the angel told Zechariah, "Because you don't believe what God says, you will not be able to talk until after the baby is born."

Zechariah sinned when he didn't believe what God told him. Did God stop loving him? No! God loved him and kept His promise. He gave Zechariah and Elizabeth a baby boy. Add figures of Zechariah (4-1), Elizabeth (4-2), baby John (4-3), and table (4-4) to Background A.

Zechariah and Elizabeth were so happy! Soon, lots of their friends and neighbors rushed over to see the baby. Add crowd (4-5). **They wanted to know what the new parents would name him.**

Ask **What do you think would be a good name for the baby? How about Malcolm or Ryan or Jamil?** Suggest some of the children's names.

Say **The people didn't pick any of those names. They all thought that the new baby would be named Zechariah, after his father.**

Zechariah heard the people talking, but he still couldn't talk to them. So he used his hands to try to get them to understand. He pointed to something to write on. Point to tablet.

This is what Zechariah wrote so everyone could see: "His name is John." Write the name on a big piece of paper or the board, and show the children as you read the words.

Key Point

Through Zechariah, God said John would give knowledge of salvation to His people in the forgiveness of sins. Through His Holy Word, God speaks to give us knowledge of salvation and forgiveness through His Son, Jesus.

Right away, God made it possible for Zechariah to talk again! With God, all things are possible. Zechariah was so happy. He sang a special song to thank God. In the song, he sang about the special job God had for baby John to do when he grew up. He sang about how John would help people get ready for our Savior, Jesus! We still sing Zechariah's song in church today. It is called the Benedictus. Have children say *Benedictus*.

Baby John grew and grew. He learned about God until it was time to do his special job of telling people that Jesus was coming to be the Savior.

God helps us get ready for Jesus too. He gives us His Holy Word, the Bible. He also gives us pastors and others to teach us what His Word says. In the Bible, God tells us that He sent Jesus to pay for our sins on the cross so we can live with Him forever.

Bible Story Review

What you do: Show the picture on the leaflet and use the questions to review the story. This will help you assess what the children understand. Then hand out Lesson Leaflet 4 and crayons.

Ask **What name did Zechariah write on the tablet?** John

How do the people look when they find out the baby's name? Surprised

What special job will baby John have when he grows up? He will help people get people ready for the Savior, Jesus.

Direct children to the activities on the leaflet.

Say **Now look at the pictures of the people in the box.** Point to sidebar pictures.

Ask **Who are they?** Read the names as you point to each picture. Use your finger to find Zechariah, Elizabeth, and baby John in the big picture.

Say **God had a special job for John. He was going to get people ready for Jesus.** Have the children turn the leaflet over and point to the pastor. **God gives us pastors and others to tell us about Jesus. This pastor is holding something. Connect the dots to find out what it is.**

Pastors teach us about Jesus from God's Word, the Bible. They tell us how God sent Jesus to pay for our sins on the cross and how God makes us His children in Baptism. Look for the crosses hiding in the picture, and color them. How many did you find?

Option: Movement activities support learning by engaging the brain and helping children process what they have heard. Do the action rhyme "The Birth of John" on page 82 of *Wiggle & Wonder* (CPH, 22-3130).

Bible Words

What you do: Read Matthew 19:26 from your Bible so the children know it is God's Word. Have the children join you in the opening rhyme.

Say **I open my Bible book up wide**
Hold your hands, palms together, in front of you.
And read the words that are inside.
Open your hands, keeping them together as an open book.
The Bible tells us (read from Bible), **"With God all things are possible."**

Ask **I wonder . . . what does that mean?** Let children say what they think.

Say It means God has all power and can do anything He wants! It means we can trust Him to keep His promises. God kept His promise and gave Zechariah and Elizabeth a baby. God made it possible for us to live with Him forever by sending Jesus to be our Savior. Isn't that Good News?

Let's clap and say "Good News! Good News!" together. Then we'll clap as we say our Bible Words. Demonstrate; then repeat with the children.

Say Good News! *Clap. Clap.* Good News! *Clap. Clap.*
"With God (*clap, clap*) all things (*clap, clap*) are possible (*clap, clap*)."

3 We Live (15 minutes)

Use these activities to help the children grow in their understanding of what the Bible story means for their lives. Choose the ones that work best with your class.

Growing through God's Word

What you do: Put a church directory with your pastor's picture, a Bible, a baptismal shell, and Communion wafers (or a picture of them) in your story bag. *Option:* Use a tablet device to take pictures of these items to show the class.

Say God had an important job for baby John. When John grew up, he would help people get ready for Jesus. John told them, "Jesus is coming! Get ready. Be sorry for your sins, and God will forgive you. He is sending Jesus to be our Savior."

God wants us to get ready for Jesus too. He helps us learn about Jesus. Let's play another guessing game to help us think of all the ways God helps us learn about Jesus and gets our hearts ready for Him. I'll say something, and you guess what I'm thinking of!

Give the clues. When children guess correctly, show the item or its picture and name it. If they can't guess the answer, show the item or picture for a clue.

Say We learn about Jesus from someone in church. This person wears a long robe with a colorful scarf on it called a stole. He reads from the Bible and tells us about Jesus. Who is he? Accept guesses. The pastor!

We learn about Jesus when we read or listen to a very special book. It tells us about God's love. It tells us that God forgives our sins because Jesus died on the cross for us. What is it? Accept guesses. The Bible!

We learn about Jesus when water is poured on us and God's Word is spoken over us. What do we call that? Accept guesses. Baptism!

We learn about Jesus when we go to the front of the church with our moms and dads and they eat and drink bread and wine. What do we call that? Accept guesses. Holy Communion!

You did a great job! We think and say and do wrong things, don't we? But God helps us to say we're sorry for our sins. There is a special part of the church service where we tell God we are sorry for our sins. After we say we are sorry, the pastor tells us that God forgives us for Jesus' sake. Someday, we will live with God in heaven.

Craft Time

What you do: Use Craft Page 4, stickers, and crayons to make a bottle-shaped book. Ahead of time, fold the pages accordion style, starting with pages 2–4 on side 2. Fold page 2 down so page 1 shows on top. Fold page 4 back. The front and back of the folded bottle book will both be yellow. Cut around the solid lines at the top of bottle to make a bottle shape. Do not cut the sides.

Starting with page 1, read the book with the children. Have them add the stickers as you read each page. On page 5, have them connect the dots to spell *John*. Have children write their names on their bottle books and color the pages, including the surprised face (page 2) and happy faces (page 4).

Paper Plus option: Give each child a 12 × 12-inch piece of white fabric and fabric markers to make a square for a baby quilt. Have children draw a picture of themselves or a baby on their square. Stitch or ask your church's sewing group or parents to stitch the squares together into a quilt; show it to the children next week. Alternately, sew each square to a pillowcase to send home with the child who made it. Use fabric paint to add the Bible Words to each square.

Snack Time

What you do: Serve graham crackers and cream cheese or frosting. Supply plastic knives. Ask children to help you prepare the snack. Tell them this means they will help get it ready. Give them each two crackers and cream cheese or frosting to make a sandwich cookie.

Live It Out

Support a mission such as the quilt campaign of Lutheran World Relief. Look at their website to learn more. Alternately, follow the directions in Paper Plus to make quilt squares, but instead of drawing babies, have the children draw pictures of your pastor and what he does to teach them about Jesus. Stitch the quilt together and give it to your pastor as a thank-you gift from your class.

4 Closing (5 minutes)

Going Home

What you do: Send take-home pages and crafts with the children.

Sing "O Jesus So Sweet, O Jesus So Mild" (*LSB* 546; CD 4) or "Jesus Loves Me, This I Know" (*LOSP*, p. 42)

Say **God sent John to help people get ready for Jesus. God gives us pastors and others to teach us from God's Word and help us get ready for Jesus.** Say "God's Word tells me about Jesus" with the children.

Pray **Dear God, thank You for giving us pastors to teach us about Jesus from Your Word, the Bible. Help us to listen to them. Amen.**

Reflection

Did the children leave class knowing that God works through people like pastors and teachers to help them learn about the Savior, Jesus? Think of a way your class can show appreciation to your pastor for sharing God's Word with you.

Draw a line to show what a pastor uses to teach us about Jesus.

Connect the dots. Whom do we hear about in the Bible?

HOLY

BIBLE

Preparing the Lesson

An Angel Visits Joseph

Matthew 1:18–25

Key Point

Just as the angel proclaimed to Joseph that Mary would bear an infant who is the Son of God, the Savior, so God proclaims to us in His Word that this same Jesus is our Savior from sin and death.

Law/**Gospel**

Relying on my own eyes and senses, I trust what is false instead of trusting that Christ is God's Son, my Savior. **God's Word gives me the truth that Jesus is Immanuel, God with me, my Savior.**

Context

In the Jewish culture, to be betrothed, or engaged, was to be 90 percent married. The other 10 percent would be consummated on the wedding night. Thus, when Joseph discovers Mary is pregnant, the Bible speaks of his plan not as "breaking off the engagement" but as a "divorce," albeit a quiet one (Matthew 1:19).

Matthew positions this story immediately after the opening genealogy, where David is in the forefront, mentioned five times. For this reason, the angel addresses Joseph as "son of David" (v. 20), a way of subtly reminding him, and us, that in Jesus, the promises to David (2 Samuel 7) are being fulfilled.

The prophecy cited in Matthew 1:23 is from Isaiah 7:14, where the prophet Isaiah calls on King Ahaz to live by faith. Isaiah first exhorts the king, "If you are not firm in faith, you will not be firm at all" (v. 9).

Commentary

Martin Luther was fond of asking which was the greater miracle: that God became a man, that a virgin conceived a child, or that Mary believed it to be so. One might add "that Mary _and Joseph_ believed it to be so."

Mary, at least, knew she had been in no man's bed. This fact, in addition to the angelic annunciation, confirmed the miracle in her mind. As Joseph watched Mary's abdomen expand, however, we can understand his doubtfulness. If anybody had reason to struggle with the truthfulness of the virgin conception, it was Joseph.

How many Josephs are there in our world? Like his namesake in the Old Testament, this New Testament Joseph is one in a million. Both of them, Jacob's son and Mary's husband, trusted that God was still on their side, even when everything around them screamed evidence to the contrary.

Old Testament Joseph is betrayed by his brothers, framed by Potiphar's wife, and swept out of the ungrateful cupbearer's memory for two whole years. New Testament Joseph finds out his fiancée is in the family way much too soon, has to flee to Egypt to escape the fury of a tyrant, and endures no telling what during the rest of his earthly years. Is God really on the side of these Josephs? They would answer, "Yes indeed, more than 'on our side.' He is Immanuel, 'God with us,' every suffering step of the way."

Paul says, "Faith comes from hearing"—not just any hearing, though, but "hearing through the word of Christ" (Romans 10:17). As one pastor vividly put it, to see God at work, you have to pluck out your eyeballs and stick them in your ears! That is, you must see through hearing. What you hear are the words of Jesus, Immanuel, who is with us and in us, ever showing His grace and mercy.

To hear an in-depth discussion of this Bible account, visit cph.org/podcast and listen to our Seeds of Faith podcast each week.

Lesson 5
An Angel Visits Joseph
Matthew 1:18–25

Connections

Bible Words
Call His name Jesus, for He will save His people from their sins. Matthew 1:21

Faith Word
Truth

Hymn
O Jesus So Sweet, O Jesus So Mild (*LSB* 546; CD 4)

Catechism
Apostles' Creed: Second Article

Take-Home Point
Jesus saves me from sin.

1 Opening (15 minutes)

Welcome Time

What you do: Set up two activity areas to build interest and readiness for the lesson. In one, set out copies of Activity Page 5 and crayons. Make copies of Activity Page Fun (below and on CD) for parents or a classroom helper. Adjust talk as necessary.

In the other activity area, set out play dough, cookie cutters, and play dishes, or bring nativity figures for the children to play with.

Play the CD from your Teacher Tools. Greet the children, give them a sticker to put on the attendance chart, and have them put their offering in the basket.

Say Hi, [Callie]. What did you do today to get ready for Sunday School? Listen to answers. **Today, you'll hear how God helped Joseph get ready to be Jesus' earthly father.**

Activity Page Fun Get a copy of Activity Page 5. Show the page to your child, and look at each picture together. If a picture shows something that is real or true, have your child color it; if it does not, tell your child to put an *X* over it. Talk about things that are true and pretend.

Say Today, you will hear how God sent an angel to Joseph in a special way. God wanted Joseph to know that Mary was telling him the truth. Listen when your teacher tells the story to find out what happened.

MATERIALS NEEDED

1 Opening	2 God Speaks	3 We Live	4 Closing
Teacher Tools Attendance chart & CD	**Teacher Tools** Poster C CD	**Student Pack** Craft Page 5 Stickers	**Teacher Tools** CD
Student Pack Attendance sticker	**Student Pack** Lesson Leaflet 5	**Other Supplies** Sprout or another puppet Yarn or ribbon Crackers, cheese & paper plates Paper Plus supplies (optional)	**Student Pack** Take-home items
Other Supplies Activity Page 5 (TG) Play dough, cookie cutters & play dishes Nativity figures (optional) Resource Page 1 (TG)	**Other Supplies** Sprout or another puppet Pillow *Joseph's Christmas Story* Arch Book (optional) Scarves (optional)		

Active Learning Set out play dough, cookie cutters, and play dishes. Have children pretend someone is coming for supper and they need to get food ready.

Say Pretend someone special is coming to your house for supper, and you are making food for that person. What will you make? Listen to answers.

Say Before Jesus came to earth as a baby, God had to help people get ready for Him. First, God sent an angel to tell Mary that she would be Jesus' mother so she could get ready. Today, you will hear how God also sent an angel to Joseph in a dream to help him get ready for Jesus. *Option:* Set out nativity figures. Have the children act out what they know of the Christmas story.

Use your classroom signal to let the children know it's time to clean up and gather for circle time. Sing a cleanup song and then a "Gathering Song" (Resource Page 1).

Gathering in God's Name

What you do: Begin with this opening. To teach about the Church Year, use the materials in the Church Year Worship Kit (see the introduction for more information).

Sing "Our Church Family" (*LOSP*, p. 11; CD 15) or another opening song

Invite the children to say the Invocation and Amen with you. Tell them "Amen" is the special word they get to say at the end of prayers, hymns, and parts of the church service.

Begin In the name of the Father and of the Son and of the Holy Spirit. Amen.

Offering Have a child bring the offering basket forward. Sing an offering song.

Pray At asterisks, have children echo your words.
Dear Jesus,* help us to learn*
how You came as a child*
to be our Savior.* Amen.*

Celebrate Birthdays, Baptism birthdays, and special occasions

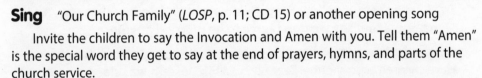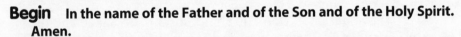

② God Speaks (20 minutes)

Story Clue

What you do: Use Sprout or another puppet. Using puppets helps to capture the children's attention, encourage interaction, and aid in language development.

Say Children, say hello to our friend Sprout. Lead children in doing this.

Sprout: Hi, Teacher. Hi, kids! I can't stay long. I'm in a hurry to see my cousin Lily. She got a pony, and guess what—it can fly!

Teacher: A pony that flies?

Sprout: Yeah, isn't that cool?

Teacher: Sprout, are you sure Lily is telling the truth?

Sprout: Well, I think so. I mean, she's my cousin, so I believe what she says.

Teacher: Children, have you ever heard of a pony that can fly? I haven't.

Sprout: Well, I'm going over there right now to find out! Bye, everyone.

Teacher and children: Bye, Sprout.

Say I wonder if Lily is telling the truth. She may be using her imagination. I know someone who always tells the truth: God! In today's Bible story, God sends an angel to tell Joseph the truth about Mary's baby.

Bible Story Time

What you do: Use Poster C, a pillow, and actions to tell the story. Encourage the children to act out the story as you tell it. Open your Bible to Matthew 1:18–25. *Option:* Use *Joseph's Christmas Story* Arch Book (CPH, 59-1546) to tell or review the Bible story.

Say The Bible tells us this true story about Joseph and Mary. They were supposed to get married. But then Mary told Joseph she was going to have a baby! She said the baby was God's Son.

Joseph loved Mary, but he didn't know what to do. He knew he was not the baby's father. He didn't think he should marry Mary anymore.

Tap forehead as though thinking. **"I know what I'll do," he thought. "I will sign papers that say we don't have to be married anymore."**

Then Joseph went to sleep. Close eyes and put head on pillow. **Zzzz. Zzzz.** Have children echo snoring. **Zzzz. Zzzz. While Joseph was sleeping, an angel appeared to him in a dream.** Show Poster C; point to angel and then to Joseph. **The angel said, "Don't be afraid, Joseph. Go ahead and take Mary as your wife. The baby boy she will have is God's Son. When the baby is born, name Him Jesus because He will save His people from their sins. This is all part of God's plan."** Put the poster down.

Then Joseph woke up. Yawn and stretch arms wide. **He knew that God had sent the angel so he would know the truth. Joseph got dressed in a hurry.** Pretend to put on clothing—pants, shirt, sandals. **He couldn't wait to do what God had told him to do. Soon after, Joseph took Mary home to be his wife, just as the angel had told him to do.**

Mary and Joseph waited for God's promise to come true. They knew the promised Savior was coming. Jesus, God's Son, would soon be born, and He would save people from their sins.

Bible Story Review

What you do: Show Poster C and ask the questions to review. Then give the children an opportunity to stand and stretch as you lead them in the action rhyme. When they sit down again, hand out Lesson Leaflet 5 and crayons.

Option: Video-record the children doing the actions in the rhyme while you read the words. Play the video for the children to watch as a review.

Ask **Who came to Joseph in a dream?** An angel

What did the angel tell Joseph? Don't be afraid; the baby Mary is having is God's Son.

Key Point

Just as the angel proclaimed to Joseph that Mary would bear an infant who is the Son of God, the Savior, so God proclaims to us in His Word that this same Jesus is our Savior from sin and death.

What did the angel say to name the baby? Jesus

Have children stand up and do this action rhyme with you.

Say **Joseph saw an angel** *Look up.*
While he was sleeping in his bed. *Rest head on hands.*
The angel had important news. *Nod head yes.*
This is what he said: *Touch lips.*
"Mary will have a baby. *Rock arms.*
Jesus, God's own Son. *Point up.*
He will be the Savior *Bow head.*
Sent for everyone." *Point to others.*
Then Joseph was happy. *Smile and clap.*
He knew God's Word was true. *Nod head yes.*
God, you see, was sending Jesus *Rock baby in arms.*
Down to earth for me and you. *Point to self and others.*

Hand out leaflets, and ask the children to put their finger on something in the Bible picture that is gold. Then they can color the circle in the sidebar gold. Do the same for the other colors. On side 2, have children color only the spaces with a dot. End the review time with the prayer on the front of the leaflet.

Bible Words

What you do: Read the Bible Words from Matthew 1:21 in the Bible.

Say **Today's Bible Words are the words the angel told Joseph in his dream. Listen while I read them: "Call His name Jesus, for He will save His people from their sins."**

Who is the angel talking about? Yes, Jesus! Let's say the Bible Words together. Say the verse together. Then divide the children into two groups. Each group will say part of the words.

Group 1: Call His name Jesus,

Group 2: for He will save His people from their sins.

Option: Whisper the first half of the verse to the first child and go clockwise around the circle. Then reverse directions. Begin with the last child and say the second half of the verse, going counterclockwise. Say the whole verse together at the end.

3 We Live (15 minutes)

Use these activities to help the children grow in their understanding of what the Bible story means for their lives. Choose the ones that work best with your class.

Growing through God's Word

What you do: Use Sprout or another puppet.

Teacher: Hey, Sprout. You're back.

Sprout: *(Sounding glum)* Oh, hi, Teacher. Hi, kids.

Teacher: Did you see Lily?

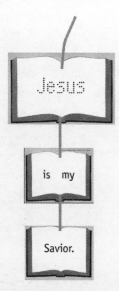

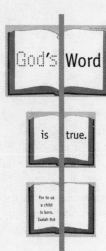

Sprout: Yeah, I saw Lily, but what I didn't see was a flying pony! Lily was just being mean and teasing me. There is no flying pony.

Teacher: That's too bad, Sprout. Unfortunately, because we're sinful, we people don't always tell the truth. Sometimes, we say things that are untrue or just pretend.

Sprout: That's for sure!

Teacher: But there is someone who does tell the truth all the time—God.

Sprout: (*Sounding happier*) Yeah, that's right!

Teacher: In our Bible story today, God sent an angel to talk to Joseph in a dream. The angel told him that Mary was going to have a baby who would be God's Son. God wanted Joseph to know that what Mary said was true. Not long after that, Mary did have a baby—Jesus. God will always give us the truth. Do you know where God talks to us, Sprout?

Sprout: (*Puzzled*) I'm not sure. In our dreams?

Teacher: Well, God can do that because He's God. But that's not where He promises to talk to us. Boys and girls, where does God promise to talk to us? (*If no one says that God speaks to us through His Word, hold up your Bible.*) What is this? Yes, a Bible. The Bible is God's Word. That is where God promises to talk to us. Everything God tells us in the Bible is true. And you know what the best truth is?

Sprout: What's that, Teacher?

Teacher: It's the truth that Jesus is our Savior!

Sprout: You're right! That is the best!

Craft Time

What you do: Give children Craft Page 5, stickers, markers, yarn, and scissors to make a two-sided mobile to hang in their room.

The mobile has "God's Word is true" on one side to remind children that God talks to us in His Word and what He says is always true. The other side says, "Jesus is my Savior." Children can use markers to trace the dots on *Jesus* and *God's.* Give them a sticker of baby Jesus to put beside the Bible verse on the Bible and a cross sticker to put on the side that talks about Jesus as their Savior. They can add the remaining stickers as decorations to either side. Punch holes in each piece, and string the pieces together with yarn to make a mobile.

Option: Instead of using yarn, give children a long piece of narrow ribbon to tape or glue to the middle of the three book pieces to hold them together. The ribbon will look like a bookmark. Punch a hole in the top book and string yarn through it to hang as a wall hanging.

Paper Plus option: Make baby peg dolls. For each doll, you'll need a 2 5/16-inch wooden peg doll (available at craft stores) and a piece of flannel material in a baby print, cut into a 5 × 5-inch square. You'll also need glue, fine-point paint markers, and paper plates.

Use markers to add the face (or leave face blank). Show the children how to swaddle their baby by wrapping the right side of the blanket around the peg baby diagonally. Then pull the bottom corner up and pull the left corner over diagonally. The baby's face will be centered in the V of the swaddled blanket. Secure blanket with a small amount of glue.

Talk about the angel's message to Joseph: Mary's baby boy would be God's Son. They were to name Him Jesus because He will save His people from their sins.

Snack Time

What you do: Give each child a round cracker and three triangle crackers (or cheese slices cut into triangles). Also give them a paper plate with a circle for the head and triangles for the body and wings of an angel. Tell the children to match their crackers to the shapes on their plates. Then say a prayer and enjoy the snack.

Live It Out

Encourage children to locate all the Bibles in their homes. Have them count how many they found and report back next week. Have them find out where the Bibles came from. How are they used? Think about sponsoring a class project of sending Bibles to the mission field.

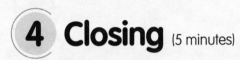 **4 Closing** (5 minutes)

Going Home

What you do: Send take-home pages and crafts with the children.

Sing "Jesus, Our Good Friend" (*LOSP,* p. 77; CD 13) or "O Jesus So Sweet, O Jesus So Mild" (*LSB* 546; CD 4)

Tell children this hymn talks about Jesus coming to earth as a baby. Have them pretend to rock a baby in their arms each time they hear the name *Jesus.* Encourage them to sing the refrain.

Say **The angel gave Joseph the truth that Mary would be the mother of our Savior, Jesus. God's Word gives us the truth that Jesus saves us from our sin. Let's say, "Jesus saves me from sin" together.** Do so.

Pray **Dear God, thank You for Your Word, the Bible. We are glad to know the truth that Jesus saves us from our sins. Help us always trust in Him. Amen.**

Reflection

What happened today to make you smile? What changes do you need to make for next week?

Color what is true (the things that are real or could happen).
Put an X on what is not true (the things that are make-believe).

Preparing the Lesson

The Birth of Jesus

Luke 2:1–20

Key Point

A Savior is born to you! He is Christ the Lord.

Law/Gospel

Because of sin, I am afraid and helpless before God and deserve to die. **God sent His Son, Jesus, to save me from sin and death, and He makes me His own dear child through faith in Him.**

Context

Luke makes sure to proclaim Jesus as a real man born in the historical events of this world. The story of Jesus is not a moralizing fable.

Commentary

The story of Jesus' birth is a real event. In the text, we see His mother, Mary, plodding along a dusty road with the discomforts of a woman in her third trimester. We can only imagine the difficulty of childbirth in those days.

We see the infant Jesus wrapped in cloths and lying in a hay-filled feeding trough. We see unnamed shepherds praising this newborn as the Savior of God's people. We see parents caught up in the drama that includes birth, blood, and humility, as well as the rejoicing of heavenly armies.

Heaven and earth meet in this baby, the swaddled Lord of all creation nursing at His mother's breast. We hear in the Scriptures how the Lord set aside His greatness to become humble. Yet through His humility, He makes the humble great and seats common folk among the greatest of the heavenly powers.

When God catches us up in His plans, we simply receive His words and the works He would have us do, and like Mary, we ponder in our hearts the greatness of our merciful Lord.

We confess that the bloody birth and death of Jesus lead us to the empty tomb and the heavenly throne, where our Lord's wounds are badges of everlasting honor and His earthly grief becomes His—and our—eternal glory. "Worthy is the Lamb who was slain" (Revelation 5:12).

To hear an in-depth discussion of this Bible account, visit cph.org/podcast and listen to our Seeds of Faith podcast each week.

The Birth of Jesus

Luke 2:1–20

Connections

Bible Words
For unto you is born . . . a Savior, who is Christ the Lord. Luke 2:11 (CD 5)

Faith Word
Savior

Hymn
O Jesus So Sweet, O Jesus So Mild (*LSB* 546; CD 4)

Catechism
Apostles' Creed: Second Article

Liturgy
Hymn of Praise: Gloria in Excelsis

Take-Home Point
God sent Jesus to be my Savior.

 Opening (15 minutes)

Welcome Time

What you do: Set up two activity areas to build interest and readiness for the lesson. In one, set out copies of Activity Page 6A, crayons, snippets of yellow yarn, and glue sticks. Make copies of Activity Page Fun (below and on CD) for parents or a classroom helper. Adjust talk as necessary.

In the other activity area, set out old Christmas cards, or blocks and unbreakable nativity figures.

Play the CD from your Teacher Tools. Greet the children, give them a sticker to put on the attendance chart, and have them put their offering in the basket.

Say Hi, [Xavier]. What is the best gift you ever got? Today, we're going to talk about the best gift in the world!

Activity Page Fun Get a copy of Activity Page 6A. Show the page to your child.

Ask Who is this? Yes, it's baby Jesus! What is He sleeping in? Tell your child that Mary put Jesus in a manger, a place that holds hay or straw for animals. **Let's put some straw in Jesus' manger.** Have your child color the manger and Jesus, and then glue snippets of yarn to the manger for straw.

Say Now connect the dots around Jesus. What do you see? It looks like a big present, doesn't it? Today, you will hear how Jesus is God's gift to us! Have your child color the bow on top of the gift box.

© 2015 Concordia Publishing House. Reproduced by permission. Available on the Teacher CD.

MATERIALS NEEDED

1 Opening	2 God Speaks	3 We Live	4 Closing
Teacher Tools Attendance chart & CD	**Teacher Tools** Storytelling Figures 6-1 to 6-7 Background A CD	**Teacher Tools** CD	**Teacher Tools** CD
Student Pack Attendance sticker	**Student Pack** Lesson Leaflet 6 & sticker	**Student Pack** Craft Page 6 Stickers	**Student Pack** Take-home materials
Other Supplies Activity Page 6A (TG) Yellow yarn & glue sticks Christmas cards or nativity figures & blocks Resource Page 1 (TG)	**Other Supplies** Nativity figure of Jesus & gift box Activity Pages 6A & 6B (TG, optional) Yarn (optional) *Baby Jesus Is Born* Arch Book (optional)	**Other Supplies** Gift box Decorative items Cupcakes Paper Plus supplies & Activity Page 6C (optional)	

Active Learning Place old Christmas cards on the table. Include cards with pictures of shepherds and angels. Have the children sort the cards into two piles. In one pile, place pictures that tell of baby Jesus, the shepherds, the angels, and so forth. In the other pile, place cards that show ornaments, decorations, reindeer, and the like.

Ask **What do these pictures tell you about? Which pictures tell about Jesus' birthday?**

Option: Set out blocks and unbreakable nativity figures. Encourage the children to build a stable and manger for baby Jesus.

Use your classroom signal to let the children know it's time to clean up and gather for circle time. Sing a cleanup song (Resource Page 1).

Say **Shh. Pretend there is a baby sleeping here. Walk as quietly as you can to the story area. You'll hear more about this special baby soon.**

Gathering in God's Name

What you do: Gather the children, and begin with this opening. To teach about the Church Year, use the materials in the Church Year Worship Kit (see the introduction for more information).

Sing "Our Church Family" (*LOSP*, p. 11; CD 15) or another opening song

Invite the children to say the Invocation and Amen with you. Tell them "Amen" is the special word they get to say at the end of prayers, hymns, and parts of the church service.

Begin **In the name of the Father and of the Son and of the Holy Spirit. Amen.**

Offering Have a child bring the offering basket forward. Sing an offering song.

Pray **Dear Jesus,* help us to learn* how You came as a child* to be our Savior.* Amen.***

*Have children echo each phrase after the asterisk.

Celebrate Birthdays, Baptism birthdays, and special occasions

② God Speaks (20 minutes)

Story Clue

What you do: Put a nativity figure of baby Jesus inside a small box, or copy the picture of Jesus in the manger on Activity Page 6A to put in the box. Wrap the box in Christmas paper or some other attractive gift wrap; wrap the lid separately so it can be re-closed. Attach a tag that reads, "To everyone." Hold the gift on your lap.

Say **Today, I brought a special gift with me. Isn't it beautiful? I wonder who it is for. Let's see what the tag says. It says, "To everyone." Hmm. What do you think is inside this gift?** Accept suggestions.

I'll give you a hint. Inside this box is the best present I ever got. It's the best present you'll ever get too. Let's open the box and see what it is. Open the box; ask a child to pull out the figure or picture of Jesus.

Say It's a figure (or picture) of Jesus! He is the best gift God gives us. Without Jesus, we would not have Christmas. Without Jesus, we would not have God's forgiveness. Let's listen to our Bible story and find out why Jesus is God's best gift.

Bible Story Time

What you do: Use Background A and the storytelling figures to teach the Bible story. Put the figures in your Bible. Use a restickable glue stick, double-stick tape, or loops of tape to attach the figures to the background when you tell the story. *Option:* Tell the story using the Arch Book *Baby Jesus Is Born* (CPH, 59-1579) or another Christmas story Arch Book.

Great Tip for Special Needs!

Visual aids help children to focus. Keep the attention of fidgety children by giving them a soft or pliable object like a woolly lamb to hold.

Ask Mary and Joseph lived in Nazareth. One day, the ruler of the country wanted to count all the people. So he told the people that they had to go back to the town where their families came from. Mary and Joseph had to go to a little town called Bethlehem. So they packed up the things they would need for their trip and started walking. Add Mary on donkey (6-1) and Joseph (6-2). **Walk, walk, walk.** Whisper: **Good news is coming!**

When they got to Bethlehem, Mary was tired. She was ready to have her baby. But Joseph could not find a place for them to stay. Knock. Knock. Knock. He and Mary looked and looked, but no one had any rooms. All the places were full of people. Finally, they found a place to sleep in a stable, a place where animals lived. Moo. Moo. Moo. Whisper: **Good news is coming!**

Near Bethlehem, some shepherds were out on the hills watching over their sheep and lambs. Replace Mary and Joseph with shepherds (6-4). **"Baa, baa, baa,"** said a little lamb. The shepherds watched over their sheep to keep other animals from hurting them. It was quiet and dark all around them. Shh. Shh. Shh. Whisper: **Good news is coming!**

Key Point

A Savior is born to you! He is Christ the Lord.

Suddenly, the sky was filled with light, and an angel appeared in front of the shepherds. Add angel (6-5). The shepherds had never seen anything like it before! They didn't know what was happening. They were afraid. Shake. Shake. Shake. Whisper: **Good news is coming!**

The angel told them, "Don't be afraid! I have good news to tell you that will bring great happiness to everyone. In Bethlehem, this very night, your Savior, Jesus, was born. He is Christ the Lord. You will find Him wrapped in baby clothes and lying in a manger." Then the sky was filled with angels singing praise to God, "Glory to God in the highest and on earth peace to men." Add two more angels (6-6). **Sing. Sing. Sing.** Whisper: **Good news is here!**

After the angels went away, the shepherds started talking to one another. Remove angels. They said, "Let's go find this baby the angels told us about!" So they hurried to the stable and found Mary and Joseph. Run. Run. Run. Add stable roof (6-3), Mary (6-7), and Joseph (6-2). And right by them, lying in a manger, was baby Jesus, just as the angels said He would be. Add baby Jesus (6-8). **How happy the shepherds were to see Him! Joy. Joy. Joy.** Whisper: **Good news is here!**

How happy the shepherds were! Here was the best present they could ever have—a Savior! Jesus would grow up and take the punishment for everyone's sins by dying on the cross and rising again on Easter.

When the shepherds went back to their sheep, they praised God and told everyone they met about Jesus. Good news! Good news! Good news! In a loud voice: **Good news! The Savior is born!**

The song the angels sang the night Jesus was born is one we still sing in church. It is the Gloria in Excelsis ("Glory to God in the highest") from Luke 2:14, which begins the Hymn of Praise in the Divine Service. Encourage the children to listen for this song when they go to church and to let you know if they hear it.

Bible Story Review

What you do: Hand out Lesson Leaflet 6, the sticker of baby Jesus, and crayons. Use the leaflet and questions to first review the story.

Option: For an active review, make photocopies of the angel and shepherd figures on Activity Page 6B. Cut them out, punch a hole in the top of each, and string yarn through it so it can be worn like a necklace. Give each child one to wear. As you retell the story, help the children act out the parts of angels and shepherds.

Ask **Who is this special baby?** Jesus

Who else do you see in the picture? Accept answers.

Who told the shepherds about Jesus' birth? The angels

What do the shepherds do when they go back to their sheep? They tell everyone they see about Jesus.

Have children look at side 1 of their leaflets. Ask them to place a finger on each of the pictures in the sidebar as you say the word describing the picture. Read from top to bottom. Have the children color just the pictures they find in the Bible story picture (the sheep and shepherds). Talk about gifts. Give the children the sticker of Jesus to add to the present to show that He is God's best gift to us.

Encourage the children to read the rebus of the Bible story on the back of the leaflet with a grown-up at home.

Bible Words

What you do: Read the Bible Words from Luke 2:11 in your Bible. Have the children join you in the opening rhyme and say the Bible Words with you, or play the Bible Words song on the CD and have them sing along. Point to the pictures on the Lesson Leaflet as you read or listen to the words.

Say **I open my Bible book up wide**
Hold your hands, palms together, in front of you.
And read the words that are inside.
Open your hands, keeping them together as an open book.
The Bible tells us:
"For unto you is born . . . a Savior, who is Christ the Lord."

Point out the pictures on the leaflet that illustrate each part of the Bible Words.

Say **God sent Jesus to be our Savior. That's Good News! Let's say those words together.** Say the Bible Words.

Option: Listen to the Bible Words on track 5 of the CD; then sing along.

③ We Live (15 minutes)

Use these activities to help the children grow in their understanding of what the Bible story means for their lives. Choose the ones that work best with your class.

Growing through God's Word

What you do: Pick up your wrapped gift box again.

Say **It's fun to get presents, isn't it? Who are some of the people who give you gifts?** Accept answers. **Your parents and grandparents and friends give you gifts to show how much they love you.**

God loves all of us too! He loves us so much that He wants us to be His children and live with Him forever. We think and do lots of bad things, though—we sin. We don't deserve God's love. But God still loves us! Take the baby Jesus figure or picture out of the gift box again.

That's why God sent His Son, Jesus, to be our Savior. Jesus was born as a little baby. He is a real person just like us. But Jesus is also true God. He has God's power and wisdom and love. Jesus came to earth to be our Savior. He obeyed God's rules and did everything right for us. Even though Jesus never sinned, He was willing to die on the cross to take the punishment for our sins. That's why Jesus is God's best gift of love for everyone. Thank You, God! Have children stand and join you in the chorus.

Say **People waited and waited, and then He came!**
Children: Jesus is born! Let's shout for joy!
He came to a stable so small and so poor.
Children: Jesus is born! Let's shout for joy!
The angels sang the glad good news.
Children: Jesus is born! Let's shout for joy!
The shepherds heard and ran to see.
Children: Jesus is born! Let's shout for joy!
And now let's tell the whole wide world:
Children: Jesus is born! Let's shout for joy!
From *Fingers Tell the Story* © 1989 CPH, p. 85.

Craft Time

What you do: Use Craft Page 6, the nativity stickers from the Sticker Page, crayons, and other decorating supplies (such as large buttons, rickrack, ribbon, and glitter pens) to make a card. Play the CD from the Teacher Tools as children work.

Give the children Craft Page 6. Have them place the nativity stickers in the stable and color the page before you fold the picture. They can color or add star stickers to the sky and personalize the outside of the card with art supplies you have on hand (buttons, rickrack, ribbon, glitter pens).

Paper Plus option: Let children make their own birthday cake for Jesus. Purchase small gift-pack containers of play dough. Give the children sequins, buttons, and other decorating supplies to "frost" their cakes. Give them candles for the top. Sing "Happy Birthday" to Jesus. *Option:* Copy Activity Page 6C for each child. Send the page home with the children, or follow the directions on the page to make a shoebox diorama of the nativity or paper puppets that children can use to act out the story of Jesus' birth.

Snack Time

What you do: Serve cupcakes on birthday napkins to celebrate Jesus' birthday, or let bring plain cupcakes and tubs of frosting and let children frost their own cupcake. Talk about celebrating Jesus' birthday at Christmas. Sing "Happy Birthday" to Jesus; then eat the cupcakes.

Live It Out

If you have permission, take a video of the children saying this week's Bible Words or the action poem in Growing through God's Word. During the week, send the video clip to their parents. If you have a welcome screen at the entrance to your church or Sunday School, ask to post the video.

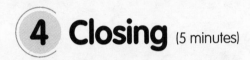 **4 Closing** (5 minutes)

Going Home

What you do: Send take-home pages and crafts with the children.

Sing "God Loves Me Dearly" (*LOSP,* p. 85; CD 10) or "O Jesus So Sweet, O Jesus So Mild" (*LSB* 546; CD 4)

Have children pretend to rock a baby in their arms each time they hear the name *Jesus.* Encourage them to sing the refrain.

Say **Today, we talked about the day Jesus was born. God sent His Son, Jesus, to be our Savior! Let's say, "God sent Jesus to be my Savior" together.** Do so.

Pray **Dear God, thank You for loving us. Thank You for sending Jesus to take away our sins. Help us remember that He is our best gift. We praise You! Amen.**

Reflection

Children like to repeat favorite songs and action rhymes. Repeating them also helps the children to learn them better. Keep your focus on the Good News message that Jesus, our Savior, was born as a baby and grew up to die and rise again to pay for our sins.

Stand-up Paper Puppet Patterns: The Christmas Story

Directions: Color and cut out the figures. Add snippets of yarn to the manger for hay and pulled-apart cotton balls to the sheep for wool. Fold Mary and Joseph figures on the dotted lines. Tape or glue all the figures to upside-down paper cups. Use as storytelling figures.

To make a diorama, color the inside of a shoebox to look like a barn. Position the puppets inside the shoebox, and tape in place.

Activity Page 6C *Growing in Christ* Early Childhood © 2007 Concordia Publishing House. Illustrations © 2002 CPH. Reproduced by permission. This page is available on the Teacher CD.

Preparing the Lesson

The Presentation of Jesus

Luke 2:22–40

Key Point

God's Law requires payment for every sin. God's Son fulfilled the Law and paid for our sin.

Law/**Gospel**

God's Law demands perfection, but I am not perfect. **As God and man, Jesus lived a perfect life to satisfy the Law in my place.**

Context

The presentation of Jesus took place in the temple in Jerusalem. This happened in order to fulfill the Law. (See Leviticus 12:2–4 for the law of purification.) The key figures are Mary and Joseph, who brought the child to the temple, and Simeon and Anna, who met the infant Jesus there.

Commentary

Jesus was circumcised on the eighth day in order to fulfill the Law. However, this cutting of skin and subsequent bleeding means more than one might think. In fulfilling the Law with the shedding of blood, Jesus set the stage for the day when He would die for the sins of the world, fulfill the whole Law, and shed the fountain of blood that gives life to every living sinner.

When the time of purification had passed (thirty-three days), Jesus was brought to the temple by Mary and Joseph. While there, they met a man named Simeon (likely an older man, possibly even near death) who was waiting for the consolation of Israel and the coming of the Messiah. Being led by the Spirit, Simeon went to the temple and there saw what his old eyes had so longed for, the Messiah. Upon taking Jesus into his arms, Simeon sang the great canticle that we call the Nunc Dimittis.

In this canticle, Simeon proclaimed that the infant in his arms, Jesus Christ, was salvation in the flesh (incarnate) that would be for all people. With that great gift, Simeon could now depart in peace. It is no coincidence that the Church sings this canticle after reception of the Lord's Supper. For, like Simeon, when we have received the very body and blood of our Lord Jesus Christ, we can depart both the altar and this life in peace, for we have not only seen salvation but have also held it in our mouths and received it into our bodies and souls.

Following the joyous canticle, Simeon spoke the solemn news concerning Jesus' destiny and the fact that a sword would pierce Mary's soul as well. One cannot be sure of this "sword," but it is likely that it could refer to, among other things, her sorrow over the betrayal, suffering, and death of her Son.

This section concludes with the prophetess Anna responding to the Good News spoken by Simeon. Simeon said that this child was the salvation of God, and Anna carried that message to all those present who were awaiting the redemption of Israel.

To hear an in-depth discussion of this Bible account, visit cph.org/podcast and listen to our Seeds of Faith podcast each week.

Lesson 7

The Presentation of Jesus

Luke 2:22–40

Connections

Bible Words
My eyes have seen Your salvation. Luke 2:30

Faith Word
Jesus

Hymns
Jesus! Name of Wondrous Love (*LSB* 900; CD 2)

Catechism
Apostles' Creed: Second and Third Articles

Liturgy
Nunc Dimittis

Take-Home Point
I will see Jesus with my own eyes in heaven.

 1 Opening (15 minutes)

Welcome Time

What you do: Set up two activity areas. In one, set out copies of Activity Page 7A and crayons. Make copies of Activity Page Fun (below and on CD) for parents or a classroom helper. Adjust talk as necessary.

In the other activity area, set up rows of chairs or benches for pews. Put out Bibles, hymnals, offering plates, old bulletins, candlesticks, and the like for the children to "play" church. *Option:* Copy Activity Page 7B and 7C for children to make a picture of things they see in church.

Play the CD from your Teacher Tools. Greet the children, give them a sticker to put on the attendance chart, and have them put their offering in the basket.

Say Hi, [Beatrice]. I wonder . . . when is your birthday? Is it hard to wait for it? How do you feel when it finally gets here? Today, we're going to talk about some people who waited a long time to see Jesus.

Activity Page Fun Get a copy of Activity Page 7A. Point to the pictures at the top of the page.

Say These little pictures are hiding in the big picture. Use your eyes to look for them. When you find them, draw a line around them; then you can color the page. You will hear more about these people in the Bible story today. Listen for their names.

MATERIALS NEEDED

1 Opening	2 God Speaks	3 We Live	4 Closing
Teacher Tools Attendance chart & CD	**Teacher Tools** Storytelling Figures 7-1 to 7-5 Background A CD	**Student Pack** Craft Page 7 Stickers	**Teacher Tools** CD
Student Pack Attendance sticker	**Student Pack** Lesson Leaflet 7	**Other Supplies** Sprout or another puppet Decorating supplies	**Student Pack** Take-home items

Other Supplies
Activity Page 7A (TG)
Hymnals, offering basket,
    bulletins & other church items
Resource Page 1 (TG)
Activity Pages 7A & 7B (optional)
	Other Supplies
	Sprout or another puppet
	Baby Jesus Visits the Temple Arch
	    Book (optional)
	Baby doll in a blanket (optional)
		Popcorn, oil, salt & popper
		Paper plates
		Glitter or sequins (optional)
		Paper Plus supplies (optional)	

Active Learning Have the children pretend they are in church. They can be acolytes lighting the candles, ushers passing out bulletins or collecting the offering, choir members singing, and the like.

Option: Give children Activity Pages 7B and 7C. Talk about things we see in church, or use your tablet device to take pictures of things we see in church to show the children. Have them color 7B; then cut out the figures and tape or glue them inside the church on 7C.

Use your classroom signal to let the children know it's time to clean up. Sing a cleanup song (Resource Page 1). Have children pretend they are walking to church as they gather for circle time.

Gathering in God's Name

What you do: Gather the children, and begin with this opening. To teach about the Church Year, use the materials in the Church Year Worship Kit.

Sing "Our Church Family" (*LOSP*, p. 11; CD 15) or another opening song

Invite the children to say the Invocation and Amen with you. Tell them "Amen" is the special word they get to say at the end of prayers, hymns, and parts of the church service.

Begin **In the name of the Father and of the Son and of the Holy Spirit. Amen.**

Offering Have a child bring the offering basket forward. Sing an offering song.

Pray **Dear Jesus,* help us to see* how You came as a child* so You could be our Savior.* Amen.***

*Have children echo each phrase after the asterisk.

Celebrate Birthdays, Baptism birthdays, and special occasions

2 God Speaks (20 minutes)

Story Clue

What you do: Use Sprout to introduce the story.

Teacher: Hello, Sprout! How was your birthday? Did you do anything special?

Sprout: It was great! I had a big party. We played games, and everyone sang to me when I blew out the candles on my cake. But the best part was opening all the presents! I had been waiting for weeks to see what was in them!

Teacher: It's hard to wait for special things; isn't it, Sprout?

Sprout: It sure is! I thought my birthday would never come!

Teacher: It is hard to wait for birthdays and other special times. The Bible tells about two of God's people who had to wait a long time too. They had been waiting their whole lives for God to send the Savior He promised.

Sprout: Wow! That is a long time to wait!

Teacher: Yes, it was. But they trusted God to keep His promise. One day, Mary and Joseph brought baby Jesus to God's house, the temple. There, an old man and woman got to see Jesus with their very own eyes. Sit here and you can listen to the story.

Bible Story Time

What you do: Use Background A and figures 7-1 to 7-5 to tell the story, or wrap a doll in a blanket (for baby Jesus) and act out the story. Directions for acting it out are in square brackets. If you use the figures, you'll need a restickable glue stick, double-stick tape, or loops of tape to attach the figures to the background. *Option:* Tell the story using *Baby Jesus Visits the Temple* Arch Book (CPH, 59-1544).

Say **Mary and Joseph called their baby Jesus. The name Jesus means "the Lord saves." The angel told them to call their baby Jesus because He would save us from our sins. When Jesus was six weeks old, Mary and Joseph took Him to God's house in Jerusalem.** [Walk in place, holding doll in arms.]

They brought an offering with them to give to God. They did this because they loved God and wanted to obey His Law. [Pretend to carry basket with offering.]

God's house, the temple, was very big. [Draw a big square with hands.] **Mary held baby Jesus as she walked beside Joseph into the temple.** If using storytelling figures, put Mary (7-1) and Jesus (7-3) on Background A. [If acting it out, walk in front of class, carrying doll.] **Joseph carried their offering for God in a cage—two little doves.** Add Joseph (7-2). **There were many other people in God's house that day. They had come to pray and give offerings to God too.**

A man named Simeon was also in God's house. Add Simeon (7-4). **Simeon knew that God had promised to send a Savior. God told Simeon that he would get to see the Savior before he died. That made Simeon very happy! Each day, Simeon wondered if that would be the day the Savior would come. Now, Simeon was very old. He had been waiting his whole life for the Savior to come.**

When Simeon saw baby Jesus, he knew right away that Jesus was the Savior God had promised to send. As quickly as he could, Simeon hurried over to Mary and Joseph and asked if he could hold this special baby. [Pretend to give doll representing Jesus to Simeon; then pretend to be Simeon taking Jesus in his arms.]

Simeon took Jesus in his arms. If using figures, add Jesus (7-3) to Simeon's arms (7-4). **Then Simeon prayed to God.** [Bow head.] **He said, "Lord, now I am ready to die because I have seen the Savior You promised to send for all people. He is a special baby. He will grow up to do big things. He will save us all from our sins." Mary and Joseph were amazed at what Simeon said. And there were more surprises to come!** [Look surprised.]

Soon, an old woman came to see baby Jesus too. [Walk in place.] **Her name was Anna.** Add Anna (7-5) to board. **Anna loved God and worshiped Him in the temple night and day. Anna was also happy to see Jesus. She thanked God for sending His Son. Then she told those around her, "This is the Savior God promised to send. He will save us from our sins."**

Simeon and Anna were so happy to see Jesus. They had waited a long time for God to keep His promise and send the Savior. They were thankful for the gift of God's Son, Jesus. [Bend down and let children peek at the baby doll, representing Jesus.]

Key Point

God's Law requires payment for every sin. God's Son fulfilled the Law and paid for our sin.

Growing in Christ

We are thankful for God's gift of Jesus too. [Nod head yes.] **God sent Jesus to earth to be our Savior. Jesus never sinned. But He died on a cross to take away our sins and rose again on Easter. Because of Jesus, God forgives our sins. Someday, we will see Jesus in heaven with our own eyes!** [Use fingers to point to your eyes.]

Bible Story Review

What you do: Give the children an opportunity to stretch as you do the action poem with them. Then hand out Lesson Leaflet 7 and crayons. Point to the leaflet art and ask the questions to review the story.

Say   **Mary picked up Jesus,** *Pretend to pick up baby.*
The Savior God had sent, *Point upward.*
Wrapped Him in His baby clothes; *Pretend to wrap a blanket around baby.*
Then to the church they went. *Pretend to carry baby as you walk in place.*

A kind old man took Jesus. *Extend arms forward, palms up.*
He held the baby small. *Pretend to cradle baby.*
He loved the baby Jesus, *Pretend to hug baby.*
Who came to save us all. *Point to classmates.*

Ask   **Where did Mary and Joseph take baby Jesus?** To the temple

Who are the old man and woman? Simeon and Anna

What is Simeon saying? He is thanking God for sending Jesus to be our Savior.

Have children look at their leaflets. Name each picture in the sidebar; then ask the children to circle the picture that shows what God promised to let Simeon see before he died. Talk about the gift of Jesus, and have the children write the first letter of their name on the gift tag and color it. On side 2, finish drawing Jesus.

Bible Words

What you do: Read the Bible Words from Luke 2:30 in your Bible. Have the children join you in the opening rhyme and say the Bible Words with you.

Say   **I open my Bible book up wide**
Hold your hands, palms together, in front of you.
And read the words that are inside.
Open your hands, keeping them together as an open book.
In God's Word, I read: "My eyes have seen Your salvation."

Simeon said these words when he saw baby Jesus. When Simeon looked at Jesus, he saw a human baby. But he also saw someone for whom he was waiting, someone who was more than just a baby. Through the power of the Holy Spirit, Simeon saw Jesus as his Savior. The Holy Spirit gave Simeon eyes of faith.

The Holy Spirit gives us eyes of faith too. Through them, we see Jesus as our Savior. God's Word shows us that Jesus kept all of God's Laws in our place and paid for our sins on the cross. Now we have God's forgiveness and eternal life. Someday, we will see Jesus with our own eyes in heaven. Let's say our Bible Words together.

Say the Bible Words. Divide the children into two groups. Have the boys pretend to be Simeon and say the first half of the verse. Have the girls pretend to be Anna and say the last half of the verse. Say it again. Then switch parts.

Liturgy Link

After Simeon saw Jesus, he was ready to die and go to heaven. He sang a special song to praise God. We sing this song in church too. It is called the Nunc Dimittis, which is Latin for "Now You are letting [us] leave." It is sung after God's people receive the bread and wine in the Lord's Supper, through which God forgives sins and helps us grow in faith. Now, we are ready to leave God's house and serve God every day. Talk about this song with the children.

③ We Live (15 minutes)

Use these activities to help the children grow in their understanding of what the Bible story means for their lives. Choose the ones that work best with your class.

Growing through God's Word

What you do: Use Sprout again.

Teacher: Hi, Sprout. Wasn't that neat that Simeon and Anna saw Jesus? (*Sprout nods.*) As soon as they saw Jesus (*put hand over eyes*), they knew He was the Savior God promised to send. That made them so happy!

Sprout: But, what *is* a savior? And why did God send Jesus to be our Savior?

Teacher: A savior is someone who rescues us from trouble.

Sprout: Oh, like the time I fell into the pool and went under the water. I was so scared! But the lifeguard rescued me. He saved me from drowning!

Teacher: Yes, the lifeguard was a savior. He saved you from drowning because you couldn't get out of the water by yourself. The Bible tells us Jesus is our Savior. We can't be God's children by ourselves because of the naughty things we think and say and do. But God loves us and wants us to be His children. So He sent Jesus to do what we can't. Jesus is God. When He came to earth, He didn't do one naughty thing. Then He died on the cross to take the punishment for our sins and came alive again. Now, we can live with God someday in heaven.

Sprout: Simeon and Anna saw Jesus with their own eyes. I wish I could too.

Teacher: Well, we don't see Jesus right now with our eyes. But Jesus promises in God's Word, the Bible, that He is with us. He is with us in Baptism where the Holy Spirit gives us faith and makes us part of God's family. Because you belong to Jesus, someday you will see Jesus in heaven with your eyes too!

Sprout: Yay! That makes me happy! (*Sprout claps; teacher nods in agreement.*)

Craft Time

What you do: Use Craft Page 7, stickers, and decorating supplies to make a viewer. *Option:* Give the children glitter or sequins for the heaven side.

Have children decorate both sides; then make it into a viewer by rolling the page into a cylinder (either side out) and taping the edge at the line. Take the children into the sanctuary to use their viewers to look for things that tell them about Jesus, or let them pretend they are in church and describe what they might see.

Say Today, we're going to make a viewer. It shows that Jesus was born to save us from our sins and that we will see Him someday in heaven! Have children point to Mary and Joseph.

Wait! Someone special is missing! We need to put baby Jesus with His mommy and daddy. Give each child a sticker of baby Jesus.

Ask Who saw baby Jesus in God's house? Give each child Anna and Simeon stickers. Review why God sent Jesus to be our Savior.

Say We can't see Jesus with our eyes right now. But because Jesus died on the cross to save us from our sins, someday everyone who believes in Jesus will live with Him in heaven. Heaven is a perfect place. There is no sin. No one is ever sick. No one is ever sad. No one ever fights in heaven. But the best part about heaven is that we will see Jesus!

Ask   What do you think heaven might look like?

Say   No one knows for sure. But the Bible says it looks like a big, fancy city made of gold. Have children turn to side 2. **Whom will we see in heaven? Yes, Jesus!**

Give children a Jesus sticker and gem stickers; have them draw themselves beside Jesus and finish the picture. Make the page into a viewer.

Say   In heaven, we will see Jesus with our eyes. Let's use our viewers to look for things that tell us about Jesus now (cross, Bible, Jesus picture, church, etc.).

Paper Plus option: Provide large sheets of poster paper (10 x 16 inches is ideal) and a variety of decorating supplies (water paints, glitter, cotton balls, foil paper, crayons, etc.). Encourage the children to make a big picture of what they think heaven looks like. "Frame" their picture by gluing it to a larger (11 x 17) piece of construction paper so the edges show around the original picture as a frame.

Snack Time

What you do: Bring an electric popcorn maker, popcorn, oil, salt, and paper plates. As the popcorn pops, talk about waiting. Is it easy or hard to wait? When it's popped, add salt and portion it out on paper plates to enjoy.

Live It Out

Encourage the children to pray for others to come to know Jesus as their Savior whenever they are waiting at a stoplight this week.

 **4 Closing** (5 minutes)

Going Home

What you do: Send take-home pages and crafts with the children.

Sing   "God Loves Me Dearly" (*LOSP,* p. 85; CD 10) or "Jesus! Name of Wondrous Love" (*LSB* 900; CD 2)

Say   God gave Simeon and Anna eyes of faith to believe in Jesus as their Savior. God gives us faith to believe in Jesus too. Because Jesus kept God's Law for us and paid for our sins, God forgives us. Someday, we will see Jesus with our own eyes in heaven. Let's say, "I will see Jesus with my own eyes in heaven." Do so.

Pray   Dear God, thank You for keeping Your promises. Thank You for sending Jesus to be our Savior. Amen.

Reflection

Which part of today's lesson did your children enjoy the most? Use similar activities (finger plays, art projects, etc.) in the next lessons to facilitate learning.

Lesson 7

Directions: Use your eyes to look for these things in the picture. When you see them, circle them.

Things I See in Church

Lesson 7

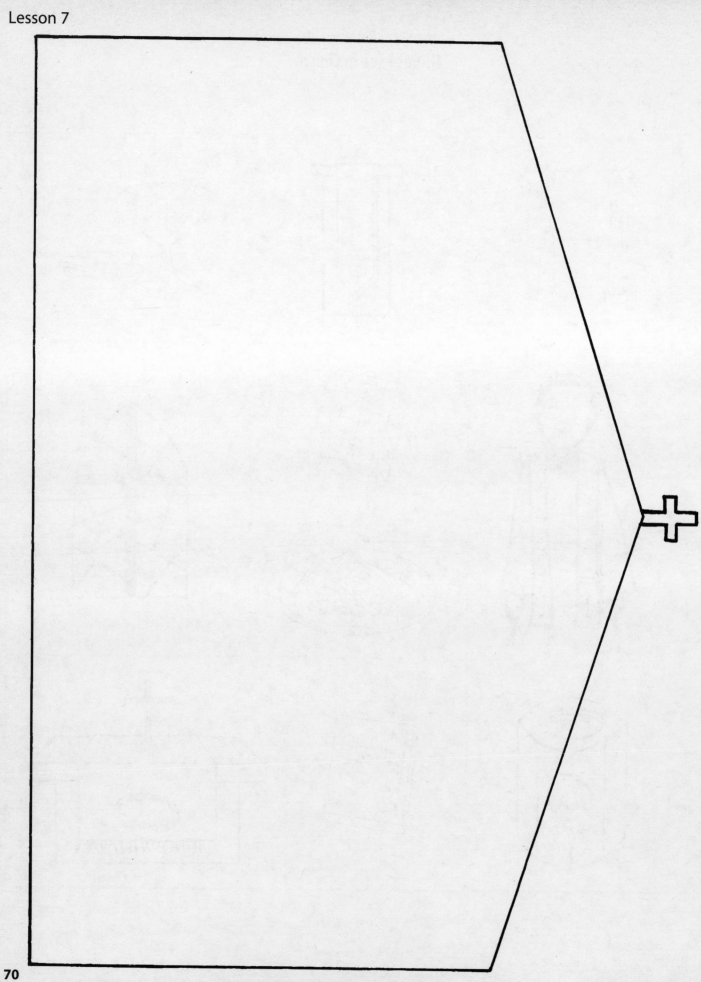

Preparing the Lesson

The Visit of the Wise Men

Matthew 2

Key Point

The Wise Men came to see the Savior and honor Him with gifts. In church, we see the Savior in His gifts of Word and Sacrament, which honor and bless us.

Law/**Gospel**

Like Herod, I do not want to worship the Savior, Jesus. **Christ comes to me, a sinner, to turn my hardened heart toward Him through His gifts of Word and Sacrament, enabling me to offer Him my worship and praise.**

Context

The visit of the Wise Men took place in Bethlehem sometime after the birth of Jesus. There is no record of exactly when the trip was made or how many Wise Men made the trip. We do know that three gifts were given.

Commentary

Matthew 2 can be divided into three sections: the visit of the Wise Men, or Magi (vv. 1–12); the flight to Egypt (vv. 13–18); and the return to Nazareth (vv. 19–23).

The first event, the visit of the Wise Men, finds its significance in the false claims of King Herod. He was not a Jew by race and has no desire to worship the one "born king of the Jews" (v. 2). Rather, this false Jew claimed a false desire to worship Jesus, while in fact longing to destroy Him (v. 13). However, even amid those who sought to destroy the Kingdom, the Gospel remained steadfast. The Gospel was found not in the spoken words of the Magi but in the quiet star that led them to Christ. That is the purpose of the Gospel: to lead to Christ and to show forth Christ.

When the star came to rest over the house in Bethlehem, the Magi entered and beheld with their eyes a sight that has long brought joy to all Christians: the blessed Virgin and the Christ Child. (Mary is often referred to as the *Theotokos*, or God-bearer, as well as the mother of God.)

What is more fascinating is how the lowly things of this world hold the most holy of things. A meager house held the Christ Child, the mouth of a sinful pastor proclaims the Holy Gospel, and our sinful mouths cradle in them the body and blood of our Lord Jesus Christ.

There is speculation as to what the three gifts represented. However, the significance comes in the fact that the Magi gave gifts at all. This lowly child was born in a stable. Yet the Magi visit and worship and bring Him gifts. That is amazing!

Then, after the Magi were warned to return home by another way, the angel of the Lord told Joseph in a dream to flee to Egypt with Mary and Jesus and remain there until told otherwise. The flight to Egypt was not only for safety reasons, but also to fulfill the words of the Lord to the prophet Hosea: "Out of Egypt I called My son" (Hosea 11:1). Moreover, this flight was an exact reversal of the flight of Moses and all of Israel. Moses fled out of Egypt to avoid the slaughter of Pharaoh. Herod stood as Pharaoh, and Jesus, the new and greater Moses, fled to Egypt to avoid his slaughter.

Finally, the angel of the Lord appeared again to Joseph in a dream and told him to go to Israel because "those who sought the child's life are dead" (Matthew 2:20). After being warned again, Joseph took Mary and Jesus to Nazareth to fulfill the word of the prophets "that He would be called a Nazarene" (v. 23).

To hear an in-depth discussion of this Bible account, visit cph.org/podcast and listen to our Seeds of Faith podcast each week.

Lesson 8

The Visit of the Wise Men
Matthew 2

Connections

Bible Words
Jesus Christ . . . is the true
God and eternal life.
1 John 5:20 (CD 7)

Faith Word
Wise Men

Hymn
Jesus! Name of Wondrous
Love (*LSB* 900; CD 2)

Catechism
Apostles' Creed: Second
Article

Take-Home Point
God gives me gifts.

 Opening (15 minutes)

Welcome Time

What you do: Set up two activity areas. In one, set out copies of Activity Page 8B and crayons. In the other area, set out play dough, a variety of star-shaped cookie cutters, and decorating items (e.g., buttons, gems, or nonmetallic glitter). Or set out Activity Page 8A and yarn, sequins, glitter glue, and crayons. Make copies of Activity Page Fun (below and on CD) for parents or a classroom helper. Adjust talk as necessary.

Play the CD from your Teacher Tools. Greet the children, give them a sticker to put on the attendance chart, and have them put their offering in the basket.

Say Hi, [Eli]. I wonder . . . do you like to look at the stars at night? Do you know the names of any of them? Today, we'll talk about a special star.

Activity Page Fun Get a copy of Activity Page 8B. Show it to your child.

Ask How many men are there? Count them.

Say Today, you will hear about these men in the Bible story. They are called the Wise Men. God put a special star in the sky to help them learn that His Son, Jesus, was born to be the Savior of all people.

Ask Can you help them find their way to Jesus? Help your child trace the path with his or her finger first and then with a crayon.

MATERIALS NEEDED

1 Opening	2 God Speaks	3 We Live	4 Closing
Teacher Tools Attendance chart & CD	**Teacher Tools** Storytelling Figures 8-1 to 8-9 Background A	**Student Pack** Craft Page 8 Stickers	**Teacher Tools** CD
Student Pack Attendance sticker	**Student Pack** Lesson Leaflet 8	**Other Supplies** Activity Page 8A (TG)	**Student Pack** Take-home items

Other Supplies
Activity Pages 8A & 8B (TG)
Art supplies
Play dough
Star-shaped cookie cutters
Resource Page 1 (TG)
	Other Supplies
	Flashlight & blue paper
	Paper cups (optional)
	Pan of cornmeal (optional)
	Star of Wonder Arch Book
	    (optional)
	Nativity set (optional)
		Gift bag, lotion or perfume, candle
		    or incense & gold jewelry
		Straws & yarn
		Star cookies/apples & cream cheese
		Rickrack, glitter & zipper bags
		    (optional)
		Paper Plus supplies (optional)	

Active Learning Encourage children to make a variety of stars using the play dough and cookie cutters or Activity Page 8A and the art supplies. Children can add buttons or gems to their play-dough stars or shake on some non-metallic glitter to make them sparkly. Challenge them to make a variety.

For Activity Page 8A, they can glue yarn to the big outline or add glitter glue or sequins for variety. *Option:* Show a short video clip of stars beforehand.

Ask **Can you make some stars? Are they the same or different?**

Say **Our stars are different. Some are big, and some are small. Some are sparkly; some are not. You are different from others too. Look at your friends in Sunday School. You have different colors of hair and skin. You are different sizes. But one thing is the same: Jesus loves all of you.**

Today, you will hear how God put a special star in the sky to show people far away that His Son, Jesus, was born to be the Savior of all people.

Use your classroom signal to let the children know it's time to clean up and gather for circle time. Sing a cleanup song (Resource Page 1).

Say **Pretend you are riding an animal to our story area today.** When children arrive, let them share what animal they rode to your area.

Gathering in God's Name

What you do: Begin with this opening. To teach about the Church Year, use the materials in the Church Year Worship Kit.

Sing "Our Church Family" (*LOSP*, p. 11; CD 15) or "We Three Kings of Orient Are," stanza 1 (find online or in a children's songbook)

Invite the children to say the Invocation and Amen with you. Tell them "Amen" is the special word they get to say at the end of prayers, hymns, and parts of the church service.

Begin **In the name of the Father and of the Son and of the Holy Spirit. Amen.**

Offering Have a child bring the offering basket forward. Sing an offering song.

Pray **Dear God,* thank You for sending Jesus* to be born as a baby.* We are happy* that He came to save us all* from our sins.* Amen.***

*Have children echo each phrase after the asterisk.

Celebrate Birthdays, Baptism birthdays, and special occasions

(2) God Speaks (20 minutes)

Story Clue

What you do: Use a flashlight to introduce the story.

Ask **What is this? Yes, a flashlight. What does a flashlight do for us?** Turn on the flashlight and make the beam of light move around the room.

Say **A flashlight helps us see. It can show us where to go, especially in the dark. In today's Bible story, God helps some men find baby Jesus. But He does not use a flashlight to show the men the way.**

Ask What do you think He used? Yes, a star!

Say There are lots of stars in the sky. God made every one of them. There are lots of people in the world. God made every one of them too. God loves everyone. He sent Jesus to be the Savior of the whole world. The Wise Men lived far away from Bethlehem, where Jesus was born. Let's find out how God used a special star to show them the way to Jesus.

Bible Story Time

What you do: Use Background A and the storytelling figures to teach the Bible story. Cover the stone wall on Background A with blue paper to represent the sky for the first part of the story. Remove it, using the stone wall for Herod's palace and Jesus' house. Use a restickable glue stick, double-stick tape, or loops of tape to attach the figures to the background. *Option:* Glue the figures to upside-down cups, and use them in a dishpan of cornmeal, or tell the story using the Arch Book *Star of Wonder* (CPH, 59-1594).

Tip: Children who have difficulty hearing should be placed close to you, where it's easy to both hear and see you as you tell the story. Remember to give directions while looking at the child and to speak in a clear, distinct manner.

Great Tip for Special Needs!

Ask Do you remember what the shepherds saw in the sky on the night Jesus was born? Angels! God sent the angels to tell the shepherds that Jesus was born. On that same night, there were some other men far, far away. These men liked to look at the stars. They knew which stars were the brightest and which were the biggest. They even knew the names of many of the stars. We call these men the Wise Men. Add Wise Men (8-1) to plain background.

When Jesus was born, God put a new star in the sky. Add star (8-2). **The Wise Men had never seen that star before. It was so big and so wonderful! "This special star means a new king has been born," they thought. "Let's follow the star and find Him."**

The Wise Men traveled for many days and many nights. Bumpety bump, they went over the roads. Add camels (8-3 and 8-4). **Finally, they came to the big city of Jerusalem. Everywhere they went, they asked, "Do you know where we can find the new baby King? We saw His star in the East and have come to worship Him."**

King Herod heard about this. Replace camels and star with Herod (8-5). **He was afraid because he did not want anyone else to be king. He asked the teachers to find out where the new king was to be born. They told him, "God's Word says He will be born in Bethlehem."**

Remove Herod. Add star (8-2), camels (8-3 and 8-4), and Wise Men (8-1). **That night, the Wise Men followed the star all the way until it stopped over the house where Jesus was living.** Remove paper to show Background A. Remove figures except for Wise Men (8-1). **The Wise Men went into the house. Jesus wasn't a baby anymore. Now he was a little boy. As soon as the Wise Men saw Jesus, they knelt down and worshiped Him.** Add Jesus and Mary (8-6).

Then they gave Jesus some special gifts: gold (8-7), **frankincense** (8-8), **and myrrh** (8-9). **These are funny gifts for a little boy, aren't they? The Wise Men gave these gifts to Jesus because they knew He was a king.**

Growing in CHRIST.

The Wise Men were from a different country far, far away, but God loved them. He put the star in the sky to lead them to Jesus. We live many, many years after Jesus was born. But God loves us too. Jesus was born to be the Savior of the whole world. He is God's gift to us!

Bible Story Review

What you do: Hand out Lesson Leaflet 8 and crayons. Point to the leaflet art and ask the questions to review the story. *Option:* Use a nativity set to review the story.

Say **Who are these men?** The Wise Men

How did they find baby Jesus? God put a star in the sky for them to follow.

What are the men doing? They are giving Jesus the gifts they brought. They are worshiping Him as the newborn king.

Option: Gather children around a nativity set, and use this poem to review the story. Point to the stable, the manger, the angels, and so forth as you name them.

Say **Here is the stable on Christmas Day.**
Here is the manger where Jesus lay.
Here are the angels dressed in white.
Here are the shepherds they told that night.
Here are the Wise Men, following the star.
Here are the camels they rode so far.
Here are the gifts the Wise Men bring.
Here is little Jesus, our Savior and King.

Have children look at side 1 of their leaflets. Point to the dot-to-dot star.

Say **Connect the dots. What did you make? Who put a star in the sky to guide the Wise Men?**

Have children count and look for the sidebar pictures in the art and color the pictures. On side 2, have them color the gifts the Wise Men brought and draw something they would give Jesus.

Bible Words

What you do: Copy, color, and cut out the large star on Activity Page 8A. Have the children say the Bible Words with you as you read them from 1 John 5:20, or play the Bible Words song on track 7 of the CD as they sing along.

Say **I open my Bible book up wide**
Hold your hands, palms together, in front of you.
And read the words that are inside.
Open your hands, keeping them together as an open book.
The Bible tells us: "Jesus Christ . . . is the true God and eternal life."

That means Jesus came to be the Savior of the whole world. Hold up star. **God put a star in the sky for the Wise Men to follow. The star led them to Jesus. God wants everyone to believe in Him so we can live forever with Him in heaven.** Hold up star, and have children follow you around the room and back to your worship area. Hold up Bible. **Let's say our Bible Words again.** Do so.

Option: Play the Bible Words song on track 7 of the CD. Hold up the star as you listen to it. Play it again, and have the children sing along.

3 We Live (15 minutes)

Use these activities to help the children grow in their understanding of what the Bible story means for their lives. Choose the ones that work best with your class.

Growing through God's Word

What you do: Put a bottle of lotion or perfume, a piece of gold jewelry, and a candle or incense in a gift bag. Hold up the star you made from Activity Page 8A. Have the children pretend to be the Wise Men traveling on camels to see Jesus as you lead them around the room with the star held high.

Say **God gave the world a special gift at Christmas. He sent baby Jesus to save us all from our sins. The Wise Men lived far, far away. God put a star in the sky to lead the Wise Men to Jesus. Pretend you are the Wise Men, following the star.** Lead children around room.

Stop and hold the star still. **We are here at Jesus' house. It's time to get off our camels.** Have children sit down.

The Wise Men brought special gifts to give baby Jesus. Show gold. **They gave Him gold. It is worth a lot of money. It is a good gift for a king.** Take out the candle or incense. **They gave Him frankincense. Frankincense is something you can burn to make the air smell good.** Take out the lotion, and let the children smell it. **They gave Him myrrh. Myrrh is a kind of special perfume that smells good. Frankincense and myrrh can also be used as medicines. The Wise Men gave Jesus their gifts and knelt down to worship Him.**

God has given us the gift of His Son too. We go to church to worship Jesus. Let's pretend we are riding our camels to church. "Ride" around the room and sit down by your worship area.

In church, God gives us more gifts! He gives us His Word, the Bible. In the Bible, God tells us that He loves us so much that He sent Jesus to be our Savior. He makes us His children in Baptism and forgives our sins. He helps our faith grow strong. Because we are God's children, we worship Him. We sing and pray. We can tell others that Jesus came to be their Savior and invite them to church so they will hear about Jesus.

Craft Time

What you do: You will need Craft Page 8, stickers, markers, scissors, glue, straws, and yarn. *Options:* Have younger children glue the craft pieces to a large piece of construction paper to make a picture instead of a mobile. Provide glitter or sequins to glue to the star. Set out rickrack or narrow ribbon for the cross. Give the children zipper bags for the cut-apart craft pieces.

Say **Tell me about the picture.** Let children tell what is happening. **Finish coloring the page. Some things are missing. What are they? The gifts and camel!** Give children stickers of these to add to the scene. Let them decorate the star.

On side 2, have the children color the gift box. Talk about how Jesus is God's gift to us. Give the children rickrack or ribbon to glue to the cross. Have them cut

Key Point

The Wise Men came to see the Savior and honor Him with gifts. In church, we see the Savior in His gifts of Word and Sacrament, which honor and bless us.

out the picture of Jesus' face and glue it to the box. Talk about the other three gifts God gives us. Cut those apart and glue to the other sections of the gift box.

To make a mobile, cut off the star section, punch a hole in it, and string it from the middle of a straw. Punch holes in the big picture, and string longer yarn through each hole to attach it to the ends of the straw so the star hangs over the Jesus picture. See illustration of completed mobile.

Paper Plus option: Make gifts. Give the children a small amount of potpourri mix to add to a square of fabric. Tie with a ribbon. Talk about the gifts the Wise Men gave Jesus.

Snack Time

What you do: Serve star-shaped cookies or apples. Cut apples in half cross-wise and point out the star formed by the seeds. Serve apple wedges with cream cheese.

Live It Out

The Wise Men worshiped Jesus and offered Him gifts. Ask your pastor if the children in your class could sing during a church service or Bible class some Sunday to offer Jesus their praise and to witness to His love. Practice ahead of time. Give the children rhythm instruments to play as they sing and make a joyful noise to the Lord.

4 Closing (5 minutes)

2, 13

Going Home

What you do: Send home take-home pages and crafts with the children. Hold up your star.

Say **God put a star in the sky to lead the Wise Men to Jesus. Jesus is God's best gift. He came to save us from our sins. Because of Jesus, God gives us many gifts: His love, His forgiveness, His Word, Baptism, and His Supper. Let's say, "God gives me gifts" together.** Do so. **The Wise Men worshiped Jesus. Let's do that too. Kneel down and we will sing a song to praise Him.**

Sing "Jesus! Name of Wondrous Love" (*LSB* 900; CD 2) or stanza 1 of "Jesus, Our Good Friend" (*LOSP*, p. 77; CD 13)

Pray **Dear Jesus, thank You for coming to save all people from their sins. We're glad you love us and died on the cross for us. Thank You for Your gift of forgiveness. We praise You, Jesus, for Your great love. Amen.**

Reflection

If you used any of the sensory activities today, did the children seem engaged? If you have hands-on learners, consider ways to incorporate more movement and senses as you teach future lessons.

Preparing the Lesson

The Boy Jesus in the Temple

Luke 2:41–52

Key Point

As a boy, Jesus was found in His Father's house. In God's house, I hear His Word, learn that Jesus is my Savior, and receive His gifts of forgiveness and salvation.

Law/**Gospel**

Because of sin, I cannot recognize who Jesus is. **Through Baptism and the power of His Word, God makes clear to me that Jesus is His Son and my Savior.**

Context

This passage contains the last of the three scenes in the "infancy narrative" of Jesus in Luke 2: His birth, His presentation at His temple, and His return to His temple.

Commentary

Jesus and His parents, Mary and Joseph, travel "up" to Jerusalem for the Feast of Passover. Jerusalem is on a high point geographically and was also the center of the Jewish religion. People then talked about going up to Jerusalem as British students today talk about going up to Oxford.

As pious Jews, Mary and Joseph did this often. But this time, something special happened: Jesus uttered His first recorded words. In doing so, Jesus revealed His true identity and purpose. He is the Lamb of God, who takes away the sin of the world. At Passover, the paschal lamb was slain at the temple. How filled with meaning is this account of the true and final Lamb of God coming to worship at the temple!

After Passover, the family began the journey back home, traveling in a caravan to provide one another with mutual aid and protection from bands of robbers, who would often hide along the roads and assault unprotected travelers. So it was not unusual for Mary and Joseph to assume early in the return trip that Jesus was running around with His friends and would eventually show up. When He didn't, they became concerned and went back to Jerusalem to hunt for Him. Imagine their anxiety!

Finally, they found Him in the temple. To their astonishment, they found their young son carrying on a learned discussion with the Bible scholars (KJV: "doctors"). They admonished Him, as one would expect. But He gave a profound answer: "Why were you looking for Me? Did you not know that I must be in My Father's house?" (v. 49). The text goes on to say that they did not understand what Jesus had said to them. Had they known His true identity, they would have gone straight to the temple to find Him instead of looking all around Jerusalem.

We are like Mary and Joseph. We understand very little of God's Word. We are slow to comprehend, and our hearts resist divine revelation. Yet despite our faults, we have a gracious God who comes to us in the person of His Son—yes, even His twelve-year-old Son—Jesus Christ. Jesus is teaching His parents, and us, that He is the temple that will be destroyed yet rebuilt in three days. He is right where He *must* be. He is in His Father's house and is doing the things of His Father. Who is His true Father? God Almighty. And what will Jesus do for His Father? He will go to the cross and die for our sins, and on the third day rise again, giving us forgiveness of sins and everlasting life.

The phrase "it is necessary," or "must," is often used in connection with the Passion of Christ. The same Greek word is used in Luke 24:7: "The Son of Man must be delivered into the hands of sinful men and be crucified and on the third day rise." The Passion of the Lamb of God purchases salvation for us.

To hear an in-depth discussion of this Bible account, visit cph.org/podcast and listen to our Seeds of Faith podcast each week.

Lesson 9

The Boy Jesus in the Temple

Luke 2:41–52

Connections

Bible Words
Whoever hears My word
and believes . . . has eternal
life. John 5:24

Faith Word
Temple

Hymn
Jesus! Name of Wondrous
Love (*LSB* 900; CD 2)

Catechism
Third Commandment
Apostles' Creed: Second
Article

Take-Home Point
I go to church to hear God's
Word and learn about
Jesus.

1 Opening (15 minutes)

Welcome Time

What you do: Set up two activity areas. In one, set out copies of Activity Page 9A and crayons. In the other area, set out blocks and hymnals, song sheets, or papers for pretend song sheets. Make copies of Activity Page Fun (below and on CD) for parents or a classroom helper. Adjust talk as necessary.

Play the CD from your Teacher Tools. Greet the children, give them a sticker to put on the attendance chart, and have them put their offering in the basket.

Say Hi, [Jasmine]. I wonder . . . do you like going to church? What is your favorite part of the service? Giving the offering? Singing? The children's message?

Activity Page Fun Get a copy of the Activity Page. Show it to your child.

Say Connect the dots. What building do you see? Yes, it's a church. The children are happy to be in God's house. Draw a smile on their faces. Look at the little pictures. Which are things the children see in church? Circle them. Today, you will hear about when Jesus went to church as a boy.

MATERIALS NEEDED

1 Opening	2 God Speaks	3 We Live	4 Closing
Teacher Tools Attendance chart & CD	**Teacher Tools** Background B Storytelling Figures 9-1 to 9-5	**Student Pack** Craft Page 9 Stickers	**Teacher Tools** CD
Student Pack Attendance sticker	**Student Pack** Lesson Leaflet 9 & sticker	**Other Supplies** Pretzels or fruit snacks, yarn & napkins	**Student Pack** Take-home items
Other Supplies Activity Page 9A (TG) Blocks Hymnals, song sheets or papers Resource Page 1 (TG)	**Other Supplies** Activity Page 9B Church picture & Bible story books Paper plates or paint-stirrer sticks Beanbag *Jesus and the Family Trip* Arch Book & O-shaped cereal (optional)	Paper Plus supplies, including Activity Page 9C (TG) (optional) Yarn (optional)	

Active Learning Give children blocks to build a church. Talk about the things you see in church. Have the children pretend that they are driving or walking to church. Give them hymnals or song sheets or paper with musical notes on it. Allow them to sing whatever songs they know; talk about how we hear about God's love for us and how we praise God in church.

Say In today's Bible story, we will hear about a time Jesus went to church.

Use your classroom signal to let the children know it's time to clean up and gather for circle time. Sing a cleanup song (Resource Page 1). Then have children pretend they are driving to church as they gather.

Gathering in God's Name

What you do: Gather the children, and begin with this opening. To teach about the Church Year, use the materials in the Church Year Worship Kit.

Sing "Our Church Family" (*LOSP*, p. 11; CD 15) or another opening song

Invite the children to say the Invocation and Amen with you. Tell them "Amen" is the special word they get to say at the end of prayers, hymns, and parts of the church service.

Begin In the name of the Father and of the Son and of the Holy Spirit. Amen.

Offering Have a child bring the offering basket forward. Sing an offering song.

Pray Thank You, God,* for giving us* the Bible.* Thank You for churches* where we can go* to hear Your Word.* Help us to listen.* Amen.*

*Have children echo each phrase after the asterisk.

Celebrate Birthdays, Baptism birthdays, and special occasions

2 God Speaks (20 minutes)

Story Clue

What you do: Have children's Bible story books, a Bible, and a picture of your church from a church directory or one you've taken on your tablet device.

Ask Do you like to hear stories? Show the children some storybooks. **Does someone read storybooks to you?** Hold up the Bible. **What is this book?**

Say Yes, it's the Bible. The Bible tells us that God loves and cares for us. It tells how He sent Jesus to be our Savior. Show the picture of your church. **Here is a picture of our church.**

Ask What do we do in church? Accept answers. Listening to children's ideas will help you better understand their thinking about church.

Say We go to church to learn about God and worship Him. In church, we listen to God's Word and hear how He loves and forgives us because of Jesus. We sing and pray. We give offerings to say thank You to Jesus.

Ask Do you think Jesus liked going to church? Let's find out. Our Bible story is about a time Jesus went to church when He was a boy.

Active Learning Idea!

Key Point

As a boy, Jesus was found in His Father's house. In God's house, I hear His Word, learn that Jesus is my Savior, and receive His gifts of forgiveness and salvation.

Bible Story Time

What you do: Use Background B, the storytelling figures for this lesson, and a restickable glue stick, double-stick tape, or loops of tape to attach the figures to the background. Copy and cut out the faces on Activity Page 9B. Glue each to a paper plate or paint-stirrer stick. Use them to lead the children on a pretend trip to the temple in Jerusalem as you walk around your room and end in the story area. Give them copies of the faces to reenact the story at home.

Option: Tell the story using the Arch Book *Jesus and the Family Trip* (CPH, item number 59-1520). Learn the story and then tell it in your own words as you show the pictures in the Arch Book. Incorporating movement as you tell the story helps capture the attention and interest of the children. Movement also helps them to process and remember the story better.

Say   The Bible (show Bible) **tells us that when Jesus was twelve years old, He went to a special celebration with His parents at God's house, the temple. The temple was in Jerusalem, a city far away from where Jesus lived. There weren't any cars or buses or trains, so people had to walk or ride a donkey to get where they wanted to go.**

Let's pretend we are walking to Jerusalem with Mary, Joseph, and Jesus. Hold up the faces and walk in place or lead the children around the room. **Finally, they got to the big city of Jerusalem. Jesus and His family went to God's house, the temple.**

Let's pretend we are in church too. Let's sit down together. Mary and Joseph and Jesus were happy to be at God's house. Can you show me a happy face? Jesus and Mary and Joseph and their family and friends worshiped God in the temple. Add Mary and Joseph (9-1) and Jesus (9-2) to Background B. **They prayed and listened to God's Word. Their sins were forgiven. When the celebration was over, the people started to walk back home. Mary and Joseph went too.** Remove figures.

Let's pretend we are walking home. Walk in place or around the room. **Jesus' parents thought Jesus was walking with His friends. That evening, they looked for Jesus, but they couldn't find Him. They asked people, "Did you see Jesus?" But no one knew where Jesus was.** Shake your head no. **So, Mary and Joseph went back to Jerusalem.** Walk in place or around the room.

When Mary and Joseph got back to Jerusalem, they looked and looked for Jesus. It had been three days since they had talked to Him! Hold up three fingers. **Where could Jesus be? Finally, they went to God's house, the temple.** Add Mary and Joseph (9-1). **How surprised they were! There was Jesus!** Add Jesus (9-3) and the teachers (9-4 and 9-5).

Jesus was sitting in God's house, the temple, listening to the teachers and priests and asking them questions. Mary ran up to Jesus and asked, "Son, where have you been? We've been looking for You everywhere! We were so worried!"

Jesus said, "Didn't you know that I have to be in My heavenly Father's house?" God the Father's house is the church. God the Father had sent Jesus to save people from their sins. Jesus wanted to be in God's house.

Mary said, "It's time to go back home." Jesus loved God. He was happy to be in God's house, but Jesus never sinned. He listened to His parents and went back home with them. Walk in place or around room.

Growing in CHRIST.

Jesus loved His parents and obeyed them. He grew bigger every day. The Bible says Jesus grew in wisdom too. That means He kept on learning about God from His Word, the Bible.

You grow bigger every day too. God also helps you grow in wisdom when you go to church and Sunday School and learn about Him from His Word. God's Word tells us that God loves us so much that He sent Jesus to be our Savior.

Bible Story Review

What you do: Show the picture on Lesson Leaflet 9, and use the questions to review the story. Give the children an opportunity to stand and stretch as you sing the song. Then hand out Lesson Leaflet 9, crayons, and stickers of Jesus. If you wish, provide O-shaped cereal or other decorations to glue to the path.

Ask **Where is Jesus?** In the temple

What is Jesus doing? Talking to the teachers; answering questions

Where do we hear God's Word and learn about Jesus? In church; at home

Sing the song to the tune of "London Bridge" and lead children in the actions.

Sing **I go to church to hear God's Word,**
Walk in place; cup hand around ear.
Hear God's Word, hear God's Word.
I go to church to hear God's Word,
To sing and praise Him.
Cup hands around mouth.

Have children sit down. Discuss the pictures in the sidebar on side 1, and have children circle the temple. Give them a sticker of Jesus to put on the Bible.

On the back, have them take the children to church by tracing the path first with their finger, and then with a crayon or by gluing O-shaped cereal to the path. Ask children whom they hear about in church; then have them trace over the word *Jesus*.

Bible Words

What you do: Read John 5:24 from your Bible. Have a beanbag to toss.

Say **Today, we heard how Jesus was in God's house. Jesus liked to hear and listen to God's Word. God tells us in His book, the Bible, that He sent Jesus to be our Savior. [Jesus says,] "Whoever hears My word and believes . . . has eternal life." Let's say those words together.** Have the children toss a beanbag to their neighbor on each word as they say the Bible Words. Repeat until everyone has had a turn to catch the beanbag. *Option:* Use this action poem from *Wiggle & Wonder* (p. 28) to introduce the Bible Words.

Say **Here is the Bible God gave me.** *Open hands like book.*
What does He tell me? Let's look and see. *Shade eyes with hand.*
[Jesus tells me,] *Open Bible and read.*
"Whoever hears My word and believes . . . *Cup hand behind ear.*
has eternal life." *Point to heaven.*

3 We Live (15 minutes)

Use these activities to help the children grow in their understanding of what the Bible story means for their lives. Choose the ones that work best with your class.

Growing through God's Word

What you do: Use a finished craft booklet to talk about parts of a church service, or have children make their own booklets first (see Craft Time) and then "read" the pages with you and add stickers as indicated.

Say The title of this book is "I Go to God's House." Read the Bible Words. We go to church to hear about God's love and how He sent Jesus to be our Savior. Let's read this book to find out what we do in God's house. Look at page 1.

Ask What are the children and mom and dad and grandma doing? (Singing a hymn)

Say We sing about God's love in church. Put a sticker of a mouth over the word *sing*. Point to picture on page 2.

Ask What are the people doing here? (Listening to God's Word)

Say We listen to Pastor [Scott] in church. He reads the Bible and tells us about Jesus. Put an ear sticker on this page. Point to picture on page 3. These people are standing up in church.

Ask What are some times we stand in church? Accept comments.

Say We often stand in church to sing or pray. We stand to tell what we believe about God in the Apostles' Creed. We say, "I believe in God the Father. I believe in God the Son. I believe in God the Holy Spirit." Put a mouth sticker on word *tell*. Point to the next picture.

Ask What are these people doing? (Praying)

Say We pray in church to ask God to forgive us. We pray to ask Him to help those who are sick. We pray to give God thanks and praise. Add a sticker of praying hands to page 4. Point to next picture.

Ask What are these people doing? (Giving an offering)

Say We give gifts in church to help others learn about Jesus. Put a hand sticker on page 5. Point to the next picture.

Ask What do you see in this picture? (A Bible, a baptismal font, and the Lord's Supper)

Say These are all special gifts that God gives us in church. They are special because God gives us forgiveness through these gifts. We can't see God's forgiveness. But we can see the Bible, the water in Baptism, and the bread and wine in the Lord's Supper with our eyes. With all these gifts, God forgives our sins. God forgives us because Jesus died on the cross for us. Put a sticker of an eye on page 6. Point to last page.

Say At the end of church, the pastor gives us God's blessing. Jesus went home from church. We go home from church too. We are happy God

Growing in CHRIST.

forgives our sins for Jesus' sake and helps us to serve Him. Put a sticker of a foot on this page.

Ask **What are some ways you can serve God by showing love this week?** Talk about the children's vocations (helping, obeying, being friends, etc.).

Craft Time

What you do: Hand out Craft Page 9, stickers, and crayons. Set out scissors. Give children crayons to finish the pictures. To assemble the book, cut the craft page in half on the solid line and fold each half on the dotted lines. Nest the pages so they are in page-number order. Staple the books through the middle or tie with yarn. Give help as needed.

To make a shape book, cut on the slanted roof lines. Do not cut the sides. Talk about the things we do in church on each page. Have children add stickers over the circled words.

Paper Plus option: Make copies of Activity Page 9C. Give the children bits of tissue paper and glue to decorate the cross. Glue or tape it to a piece of construction paper. Trim as needed. Roll the ends of the paper toward the center to make scrolls. Tell the children that when Jesus went to the temple, the teachers read God's Word from big scrolls instead of books. They can "read" their scroll and tell how Jesus came to save us from our sins by dying on the cross for us.

Snack Time

What you do: Put pretzels or fruit snacks in paper napkins and tie them with yarn into bundles for the children. Talk about how people in Bible times didn't have restaurants. They had to carry and cook their own food when they traveled.

Live It Out

Get permission for the children in your class to do an age-appropriate service project at church. For example, they could dust pews, water plants, or recycle old bulletins.

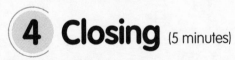 **4 Closing** (5 minutes)

Going Home

What you do: Send home take-home pages and crafts with the children.

Say **We go to church to hear God's Word. We learn about Jesus, our Savior, who died to take away our sins. Let's say, "I go to church to hear God's Word and learn about Jesus."** Do so.

Sing "We Are in God's House Today" (*LOSP*, p. 12) or "Jesus! Name of Wondrous Love" (*LSB* 900; CD 2)

Pray **Dear God, thank You for church. Help us want to go to Your house to sing and pray and learn more about Jesus, our Savior. Amen.**

Reflection

Did children gain a sense of the value of going to church? During the weeks ahead, consider ways to help them participate in worship.

Lesson 9

Connect the dots. Where are the children? They are happy to be in church.
Put a smile on each face. Circle the things they see in church.

Activity Page 9A Growing in Christ® Early Childhood © 2006, 2008 Concordia Publishing House. Reproduced by permission. This page is available on the Teacher CD.

Directions: Enlarge, cut out, and glue or tape the faces to paper plates or paint-stirrer sticks to make storytelling puppets.

[Jesus says,] " Whoever hears My word and believes . . . has eternal life."
John 5:24

Lesson 10

_____
Date of Use

Preparing the Lesson

John Prepares the Way

Matthew 3:1–12

Key Point

As John pointed to Jesus as the Lamb of God, so our pastors point us to this same Jesus, who grants us forgiveness, life, and salvation.

Law/**Gospel**

Sin hardens my heart against God, and I try to earn my salvation. **God's Word works in my hardened heart, causing me to repent and believe in the Savior.**

Context

Matthew's Gospel gives no exact date for the phrase "In those days" (3:1). However, Luke's Gospel puts the event in its chronological perspective. This event likely took place when Jesus was about thirty years old. According to Luke's Gospel, the Baptisms done by John took place in the "region around the Jordan" (Luke 3:3).

Commentary

All of the prophets had come and gone, and John was the final link from the Old Testament prophetic line to Jesus Christ. He brought the same message as all the prophets before him, but his was made manifest in the person of Jesus. He, unlike any other prophet, could point and say, "Behold, the Lamb of God" (John 1:29).

In Matthew's Gospel, John is introduced through his message: "Repent, for the kingdom of heaven is at hand" (3:2). *Repent* can mean "turn away from one's sins," but it also has the stronger meaning of being turned away from unbelief to faith or being turned from the inborn sickness of sin to the life and health that come from God through His Son.

Thus, John's preaching of repentance led many to receive his Baptism "for the forgiveness of sins" (Luke 3:3). John also intended his Baptism to produce further repentance. So repentance, along with confessing sins, leads to John's Baptism, and that Baptism leads to and produces more repentance.

Many Pharisees and Sadducees also came to him; they, however, did not repent in their hearts and turn to God. John called these hypocrites a "brood of vipers" (Matthew 3:7). Although they came for his Baptism, they did not believe or continue in the message of repentance preached by John.

Bloodlines do not get a person into the kingdom of God (Matthew 3:9), but only the succession of faith. That is how children of Abraham are born—not by flesh and blood, but through faith in the promises of God. Even today, children of pious church families are not heirs of eternal life simply by birth, but only through faith in Jesus Christ.

Those who do not have faith in Jesus Christ, regardless of bloodlines, will be subjected to His "winnowing fork" and "unquenchable fire" (Matthew 3:12). For Christ will soon come again as our judge, and He will clear the floor of all people. The faithful will receive the blessing of Christ's barn (Matthew 3:12) as they live in His kingdom forever, but the unfaithful will receive everlasting death.

The words of Matthew 3 seem harsh, but the greater message is that "the Lamb of God, who takes away the sin of the world" (John 1:29), came for all humanity. That is the message for God's people today: the Lamb of God comes to us. He comes in Word and Sacrament, and by His grace and favor, we believe, repent, and are forgiven for Jesus' sake!

To hear an in-depth discussion of this Bible account, visit cph.org/podcast and listen to our Seeds of Faith podcast each week.

Lesson 10

John Prepares the Way

Matthew 3:1–12

Connections

Bible Words
Behold, the Lamb of God, who takes away the sin of the world! John 1:29

Faith Word
Prepare

Hymn
Go, My Children, with My Blessing (*LSB* 922; CD 1)

Catechism
Apostles' Creed:
Second Article

Holy Baptism

Liturgy
Confession of Sins

Take-Home Point
Jesus is the Lamb of God who takes away my sins.

1 Opening (15 minutes)

Welcome Time

What you do: Set up two activity areas. In one, set out copies of Activity Page 10 and crayons. In the other area, set out a dishpan of soapy water and play dishes. Make copies of Activity Page Fun (below and on CD) for parents or a classroom helper. Adjust talk as necessary.

Play the CD from your Teacher Tools. Greet the children, give them a sticker to put on the attendance chart, and have them put their offering in the basket.

Say   Hi, [Hector]. I'm glad you are here! Are you ready to learn more about Jesus and His love today? Get the child started in one of the activities.

Activity Page Fun Get a copy of the Activity Page. Show it to your child.

Ask   What did you do to get ready for Sunday School this morning? Do any of these pictures look like things you did? Color the ones that do. Have your child color the things he or she did this morning to get ready for Sunday School.

Say   Today, you will hear a story from God's Word about John. God sent John to help people prepare, or get ready, for Jesus. He told them to be sorry for their sins. Listen to the Bible story, and you can tell me about it later.

MATERIALS NEEDED

1 Opening	2 God Speaks	3 We Live	4 Closing
Teacher Tools Attendance chart & CD	**Teacher Tools** Poster D	**Student Pack** Craft Page 10 Stickers	**Teacher Tools** CD
Student Pack Attendance sticker	**Student Pack** Lesson Leaflet 10	**Other Supplies** Sprout or another puppet Map or hand-drawn map Yarn Fruit kabobs/crackers & cheese Cotton balls (optional) Paper Plus supplies (optional)	**Student Pack** Take-home items
Other Supplies Activity Page 10 (TG) Dishpan, dishes, detergent Resource Page 1 (TG)	**Other Supplies** Baking items Story bag or paper bag		

Active Learning Set out a dishpan of water and some play dishes. Put a little dish detergent in the water to make it soapy. As the children "wash" the dishes, talk about how water washes away dirt and makes things clean.

Say **God sent John to help people get ready for Jesus. John told them to repent, or be sorry for, their sins. He baptized them to wash away their sins.**

Use your classroom signal to let the children know it's time to clean up and gather for circle time. Sing a cleanup song; then do a wiggles-out rhyme with the children (Resource Page 1).

Gathering in God's Name

What you do: Gather the children, and begin with this opening. To teach about the Church Year, use the materials in the Church Year Worship Kit.

Sing "I Was Baptized" (*LOSP*, p. 97; CD 12), "Our Church Family" (*LOSP*, p. 11; CD 15), or another opening song

Invite the children to say the Invocation and Amen with you. Tell them "Amen" is the special word they get to say at the end of prayers, hymns, and parts of the church service.

Begin **In the name of the Father and of the Son and of the Holy Spirit. Amen.**

Offering Have a child bring the offering basket forward. Sing an offering song.

Pray **Dear God, thank You for sending Jesus to be our Savior. Help us listen and learn today. In Jesus' name we pray. Amen.**

Celebrate Birthdays, Baptism birthdays, and special occasions

2 God Speaks (20 minutes)

Story Clue

What you do: Have a paper bag or your story bag with a few items you would use in baking. Include a bowl and spoon, cupcake papers, and a baking pan.

Say **When I get home today, I have to get ready, or prepare, for company. I put some things in my bag so I can make something good for them to eat.** Take out items, and let children guess what you will make.

Today, we will hear about a man God sent to get people ready for Jesus.

Tell children you want them to get ready, or prepare, for listening by shaking out some wiggles. Have them wiggle their toes, their knees, their tummies, and their arms, and then wiggle themselves to a seated position. Once seated, have them wiggle their fingers and place them in their laps. *Option:* Do this poem from *Wiggle & Wonder* (p. 10), encouraging the children to do the suggested actions.

Say **Let's get ready to listen. Listen and do what I say.**
Wiggle your fingers way up high.
Wiggle your fingers way down low.
Wiggle your fingers into your lap.
Then fold them quietly—just so.

Key Point

As John pointed to Jesus as the Lamb of God, so our pastors point us to this same Jesus, who grants us forgiveness, life, and salvation.

Bible Story Time

What you do: Use Poster D and your Bible. Have children say and do the story actions.

Say Today's Bible story (open Bible) **is about a man named John and the important work God gave him to do. God wanted John to help get people ready for the Savior God promised to send.**

Ask Can you clap your hands with me and say, "God sent John to do special work"? Lead children in repeating the word and actions.

Say **John lived by the Jordan River. John wore clothes made from camel's hair, and he had a leather belt around his waist. He ate locusts and wild honey.** Pretend to eat. **Many people came to hear John preach.** Point to John and the crowd on Poster D.

Clap your hands with me and say, "John did God's work!"

John told people, "You are not living as God's children. Be sorry for your sins, and ask God to forgive you. Get ready. The Savior God promised to send will be here soon."

Some of the people who heard John listened. They were sorry they had done wrong things. They asked John to baptize them, and he did.

One time, some church leaders came to see John. They wanted to know if John was the Savior God promised to send. John told them, "I am not the Savior. I am the one who helps people get ready for the Savior."

Clap your hands with me and say, "Get ready for the Savior."

The next day, John saw Jesus walking by. John pointed to Jesus and said, "Look! There is the Lamb of God, who takes away the sin of the world!"

Ask Whom was John was pointing to? Let children answer.

Say **Jesus is the Savior God promised to send to take away our sins. He is greater than anyone. He is God's Son. John was doing the work God had given him to do. He was getting the people ready for Jesus.**

Before Jesus came, God's people used to sacrifice lambs to God when they were sorry for their sins. John called Jesus the Lamb of God. We know Jesus is a person, not a lamb. But the Bible calls Jesus the Lamb of God because Jesus is God's Son who came to die on the cross to pay for the sins of the whole world.

Clap your hands and say with me, "Thank You, Jesus, for taking away my sins!" Have children repeat sentence with you.

Bible Story Review

What you do: Show Poster D to the children. Ask these questions to review. Have leaflets and crayons ready to hand out.

Ask **Who are these people?** John and people who came to listen to him and be baptized.

Where are they? By the Jordan River

Whom is John telling the people about? Jesus

Growing in CHRIST.

Give the children Lesson Leaflet 10 and crayons. Help the children identify and circle Jesus as the one John told about. They can color the pictures in the sidebar. On side 2, have them trace the dots of Jesus' robe.

Option: Do this action poem together.

Say **Follow Jesus every day.** *Walk in place.*
Listen to His words and say: *Cup hand behind ear.*
Jesus took my sins away. *Throw out your arms on "away."*
Thank You, Jesus! *Fold your hands and bow your head.*

Bible Words

What you do: Read the Bible Words from John 1:29 in the Bible: "Behold, the Lamb of God, who takes away the sin of the world!" Use the activity to help the children learn the verse.

Say **God gave John the special job of helping others get ready for Jesus. John pointed to Jesus and said, "Behold, the Lamb of God, who takes away the sin of the world!" Let's say those words together.**

Use the Bible rhyme from *Wiggle & Wonder* (p. 28) to introduce the Bible Words.

Say **Here is the Bible God gave to me.** *Open hands like book.*
What does He tell me? Let's look and see. *Shade eyes with hand.*
God's Word says: *Open hands like book.*
"Behold, the Lamb of God, *Point.*
who takes away the sin of the world!" *Make cross with fingers.*

3 We Live (15 minutes)

Use these activities to help the children grow in their understanding of what the Bible story means for their lives. Choose the ones that work best with your class.

Growing through God's Word

What you do: Have Sprout hold a map of some sort.

Teacher: Hi, Sprout! What do you have in your hand?

Sprout: I have a map.

Teacher: A map can be very useful! Do you know what a map does?

Sprout: Hmm, not exactly.

Teacher: A map shows you how to get somewhere or helps you find a place. If you want to go to another town or city, a map shows you how to get there. It shows you what roads to take. That's what all the lines are for.

Sprout: Do you have a map that shows the way to heaven? That's where I really want to go.

Teacher: No, Sprout, you don't need a map to go to heaven. God tells us how to get there.

Sprout: Really? What does He say?

Teacher: Remember in our story today? John pointed to Jesus and said He was the One who came to save us from our sins. Because we are sinful, we can't believe in Jesus by ourselves. So God gives us His Word and Holy Baptism. He gives us pastors to teach us what God's Word says and to baptize people. Pastors help people learn about Jesus and become His followers. To be a follower of Jesus means that you believe Jesus is your Savior.

Sprout: So we don't need to follow a map to get to heaven! We only need to believe in Jesus?

Teacher: That's right, Sprout. Jesus is the way to heaven. Jesus takes away the sin of the world. He promises that all who believe in Him as their Savior will live with Him in heaven someday.

Option: Invite your pastor to come to class to talk about what he does and to do this activity with children. If he is not available, gather at your classroom altar.

Tell the children that John helped people get ready for Jesus by telling them to be sorry for their sins. He pointed to Jesus and said He takes the sins of the world. Talk about the Confession and Absolution that we say in church. Then lead the children in an "I'm sorry" responsive prayer.

Teacher: Sometimes, I don't want to go to church to learn about You.

Children: Jesus, I am sorry. Please forgive me.

Teacher: Sometimes, I fight with my friend and call my friend bad names.

Children: Jesus, I am sorry. Please forgive me.

Continue with several other petitions. Conclude:

Teacher: Thank You, Jesus, for coming to take away my sins. Thank You for forgiving me. Amen.

Craft Time

What you do: Use Craft Page 10, stickers, crayons, and yarn to make a banner. Provide cotton balls, if desired, to glue to the lamb. *Option:* Show a picture of the Agnus Dei in art, or search online for a picture of the Agnus Dei to show children.

Say God's people used to sacrifice lambs to God when they were sorry for their sins. When John saw Jesus, He said Jesus is the Lamb of God. Is Jesus a real lamb? No, He is a person. He is God's Son. But the Bible says Jesus is the Lamb of God because He died on the cross to pay for the sins of the whole world. Here is a picture of how artists sometimes show Jesus as the Lamb of God, holding a flag to show He won the victory over sin for us. Show picture of the Agnus Dei.

Today, you will make a banner to hang in your room at home. Your banner has a picture of a lamb and a cross on it. The words on it say, "The Lamb of God, who takes away the sin of the world." Let's put a sticker of Jesus on this side to remind us that Jesus is the Lamb of God.

On the other side of the banner is a church. John told people to be sorry for their sins because Jesus was coming to be their Savior.

Ask When we go to church, who tells us about Jesus? (The pastor)

Say The pastor reads God's Word. He tells us to be sorry for our sins. Then he tells us that God forgives our sins because of Jesus, who paid

Growing in CHRiST

for them on the cross. The pastor also baptizes people. Through Baptism, God forgives our sins and makes us part of His family. Let's add a girl and boy and some footsteps to show they are going to church.

Have the children color both sides. Give them a sticker of Jesus to add to the lamb and stickers of children and footsteps to add to the church. Talk about how God tells us about Jesus and forgives our sins through His Word (point to Bible), Baptism (point to the font), and the Lord's Supper (point to Communionware).

Paper Plus option: After the children have colored both sides, give them cotton balls to glue to the lamb. Use a glue stick to outline the cross in glue, and have the children add yarn. Punch two holes at the top of the banner. Tie a length of yarn in each hole so the children can hang their banner at home.

Snack Time

What you do: Serve fruit kabobs or crackers and cheese. For fruit kabobs, set out small wooden skewers, paper plates, and two or three types of fruit in bowls (e.g., strawberry halves, grapes, banana slices). If you use crackers and cheese, set them out along with napkins.

Have children help you prepare the snack. Use three simple directions for them to follow, such as, take a cracker, add a piece of cheese, and put it on a napkin; or take a skewer (or stick), put three pieces of fruit on it, and put it on a plate.

Live It Out

Discuss the places children go (e.g., the library, the grocery store, church, the park), and enlist their help to draw the places on newsprint to create a neighborhood map, or ask them to bring pictures of the places they go and the people they see during the week. Glue these to the map. Talk about how we can share God's love in Jesus with our family and friends. Pray for pastors and missionaries who point us to Jesus as the Lamb of God, who takes away our sins.

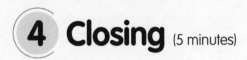

4 Closing (5 minutes)

Going Home

What you do: Send take-home pages and crafts with the children.

Sing "Go, My Children, with My Blessing" (*LOSP,* p. 922; CD 1) or "God Loves Me Dearly" (*LOSP,* p. 85; CD 10)

Say **Jesus came to earth to die on the cross and to take away our sins. He is the Lamb of God, who takes away my sins . Let's say that together.** Do so.

Pray **Dear Jesus, thank You for pastors and others who teach us about You. Thank You for coming to be our Savior. Help us to be sorry for our sins and to follow You. In Your name we pray. Amen.**

Reflection

The goal of this lesson and all lessons is to point the children to the cross and their salvation in Jesus. Pray that God would bless your words each week.

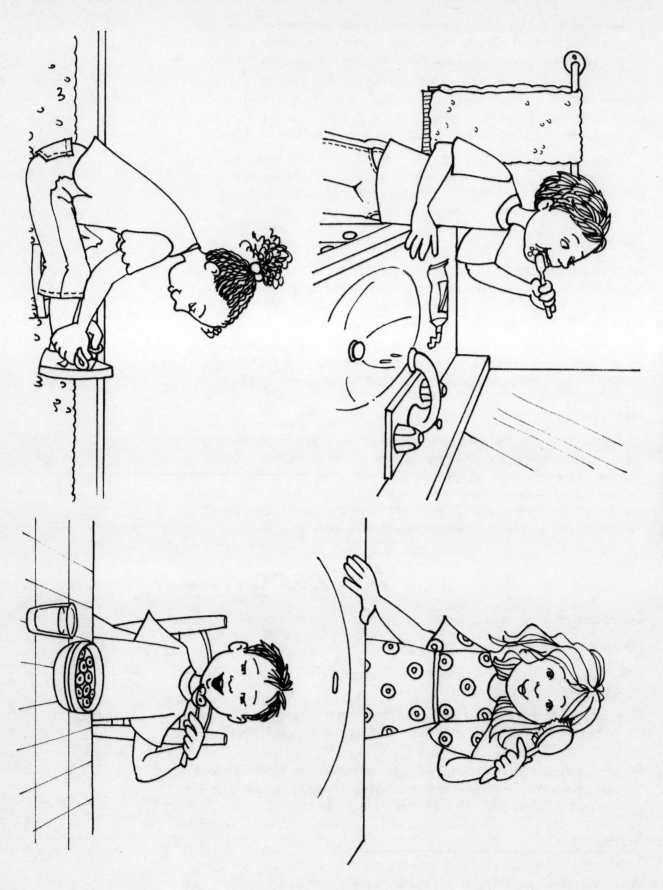

We get ready for Sunday School.

Lesson 11

Preparing the Lesson

The Baptism of Jesus

Luke 3:15–22

Key Point

Jesus was baptized "to fulfill all righteousness" so that our Baptism might give us forgiveness of sins and rescue us from death and the devil.

Law/**Gospel**

Because of God's wrath and anger over sin, I and all people need a Savior. **In Baptism, I am made a child of the heavenly Father and an heir of heaven.**

Context

John the Baptizer has been preaching repentance and baptizing in the Jordan. Now, sinless Jesus presents Himself for Baptism in order "to fulfill all righteousness" (Matthew 3:15). God the Father acknowledges that Jesus is His Son, and the Spirit descends like a dove. In Baptism, our sins become His, and His righteousness becomes ours.

Commentary

The people were in great anticipation. There had been no prophet in Israel for four hundred years. Might John be the promised Messiah? But John said no. Rather, he was "the voice of one crying in the wilderness: 'Prepare the way of the Lord'" (Luke 3:4). His work was to call people to repentance and to preach "good news" to them (v. 18). And so, John went into the region around the Jordan, "proclaiming a baptism of repentance for the forgiveness of sins" (v. 3).

John told the people that the coming Messiah was a righteous judge who would separate the wheat from the chaff—the good from the evil—at the end of the world (v. 17). While John baptized with water, the Messiah would be mightier than John. He would baptize them "with the Holy Spirit and fire" (v. 16).

But first, Jesus would Himself undergo this Baptism. So, even though Jesus was without sin, He came forward and underwent John's Baptism in order "to fulfill all righteousness" (Matthew 3:15). Jesus did not need to be baptized, but by doing so, He sanctified the waters of the Jordan and the waters of every Baptism.

Jesus had come to take on the sin of the world. By entering the waters set apart for sinners, Christ made Himself to stand as one of them. This alignment with sinners in His Baptism was the beginning of the road to the end. Here, He is baptized with the Holy Spirit in the Jordan. At the cross, He would undergo the destroying fire of God's wrath for sin.

Now all the benefits of Christ's death and resurrection are sealed to you in Baptism. You receive the gift of the Holy Spirit. In Baptism, Christ takes you through the fire with Him as you are killed, buried, and raised again to new life.

All four Gospels describe the Baptism of Jesus. Luke is unique in putting it in the past tense. Why? His focus is not just on the person of John or on the act of Baptism. His focus is on the other two persons of the Holy Trinity, who attest to the messianic identity of Jesus.

First, we see the Holy Spirit descend on Jesus "in bodily form, like a dove" (v. 22). Why a dove? Of all animals, it represents peace. A dove with an olive branch told Noah that God's wrath in the flood was ended. Thus the Holy Spirit comes upon Jesus and remains. The word *Messiah* means "anointed." Old Testament kings were anointed with oil. But the Messiah is anointed with the Holy Spirit, as this passage shows.

Then comes the voice of God the Father from heaven, saying, "You are My beloved Son; with You I am well pleased" (v. 22). God acknowledges the divine and human natures of His only-begotten Son with words similar to those He would utter at the transfiguration (9:35). Who can doubt the doctrine of the Trinity when we have such a clear passage in which all three persons are present yet functioning in distinct ways? To each person who is baptized into Christ, God says, "You are My beloved child."

To hear an in-depth discussion of this Bible account, visit cph.org/podcast and listen to our Seeds of Faith podcast each week.

Lesson 11

The Baptism of Jesus
Luke 3:15–22

Connections

Bible Words
I have called you by name, you are Mine. Isaiah 43:1

Faith Word
Baptism

Hymns
Go, My Children, with My Blessing (*LSB* 922; CD 1)

Catechism
Holy Baptism

Liturgy
Sign of the Cross

Take-Home Point
God makes me His child in Baptism.

 Opening (15 minutes)

Welcome Time

What you do: Set up two activity areas. In one, set out copies of Activity Page 11A and crayons. In the other area, set out a dishpan with water, seashells, and items your church uses in Baptism ceremonies (e.g., a candle, Baptism cloth, shell, banner, certificate, photos). *Option:* Make a short video story or PowerPoint slide show of baptismal mementos and a Baptism in your church to show the children. Make copies of Activity Page Fun (below and on CD) for parents or a classroom helper. Adjust talk as necessary.

Play the CD from your Teacher Tools. Greet the children, give them a sticker to put on the attendance chart, and have them put their offering in the basket.

Say Hi, [Deshaun]. Do you like birthdays? Today, we're going to talk about a special kind of birthday. Direct the child to an activity.

Activity Page Fun Get a copy of the Activity Page 11A.

Ask What is the little girl doing? Blowing out candles. What is she celebrating? Her birthday! Do you like to celebrate birthdays? Let child tell. Birthdays are happy times, aren't they? What do you like best about them?

There is something hidden in this picture that reminds us of another type of birthday. Can you find it? Have your child find shells.

Pastors use a shell to scoop up water at Baptisms. Baptism is another kind of birthday. In Baptism, God washes away our sin and says we belong to Him. Today, you will hear about the time Jesus was baptized. Listen to find out what God said.

MATERIALS NEEDED

1 Opening	2 God Speaks	3 We Live	4 Closing
Teacher Tools Attendance chart & CD	**Teacher Tools** Poster E	**Teacher Tools** CD	**Teacher Tools** CD
Student Pack Attendance sticker	**Student Pack** Lesson Leaflet 11 Stickers	**Student Pack** Craft Page 11 & stickers	**Student Pack** Take-home materials
Other Supplies Activity Page 11A (TG) Dishpan of water Seashells Baptismal items Resource Page 1 (TG)	**Other Supplies** Book	**Other Supplies** Yarn & art supplies Sprout or another puppet Activity Pages 11B & 11C Tissue paper & ribbon Lemonade mix & water Paper Plus supplies (optional)	

Active Learning Add seashells to the water. Let the children scoop the shells out and return them to the water. On a nearby table, set out the baptismal items. Help the children identify what they are and how they are used.

Option: Play the video you made of baptismal items and/or a Baptism, or take children to the church sanctuary to see the baptismal font. Talk about how God calls us by name and washes away our sins when we are baptized. Tell children that today they will hear about Jesus' Baptism.

Use your classroom signal to let the children know it's time to clean up and gather for circle time. Sing a cleanup song; then do a wiggles-out rhyme with the children (Resource Page 1).

Gathering in God's Name

What you do: Gather the children, and begin with this opening. To teach about the Church Year, use the materials in the Church Year Worship Kit.

Sing "I Was Baptized" (*LOSP*, p. 97; CD 12) or "Our Church Family" (*LOSP*, p. 11; CD 15)

Invite the children to say the Invocation and Amen with you. Tell them "Amen" is the special word they get to say at the end of prayers, and the like.

Begin **In the name of the Father and of the Son and of the Holy Spirit. Amen.**

Offering Have a child bring the offering basket forward. Sing an offering song.

Pray **Dear Father, thank You for sending Jesus to be our Savior. Thank You for making us part of Your Church family through Baptism and Your Word. In Jesus' name we pray. Amen.**

Celebrate Birthdays, Baptism birthdays, and special occasions

Liturgy Link

Luther encourages believers to make the sign of the cross as a reminder that they are baptized children of God. Show the children how to make the sign of the cross when you say the Invocation.

② God Speaks (20 minutes)

Story Clue

What you do: Show children a book with your name written in it.

Ask **What do I have in my hand today? Yes, it's a book. Whom do you think this book belongs to? How can you tell? Let's look inside it and see.** Open the cover to reveal your name; point it out to the children.

Say **Look. This book has my name on it. That means it belongs to me. I put my name in the book so that anyone who picks it up will see my name and know it belongs to me.**

Ask **Can you think of some things you have that have your name on them?** Give the children time to answer.

Say **Someone, maybe your mom or dad, put your name on those things so everyone would know they belong to you. It helps to keep them from getting lost. Maybe your name is on your coat or a backpack or your storybooks at home.**

In our story today, we are going to hear about a time that God called Jesus by name. God wanted everyone to know that Jesus is His Son and that God had sent Jesus to begin His special work of being our Savior.

Key Point

Jesus was baptized to "fulfill all righteousness" so that our Baptism might give us forgiveness of sins and rescue us from death and the devil.

Bible Story Time

What you do: Use Poster E, folded or cut into thirds. Show one picture at a time. Show your Bible. Remind children that this is a true story from God's Word, the Bible. *Note:* If you have children who are not baptized, reassure them that God loves them too. Speak to the pastor about them so he can talk to their families. Pray for them, and encourage their parents to have their children baptized.

Say Jesus was born as a little baby. But Jesus didn't stay little. He grew bigger and bigger, just like you do. Finally, He was a grown man. Now it was time for Jesus to do a special job. It was time for Him to show people that He was God's Son, the One God sent to save us. To do that, He had to keep all of God's Laws, and He had to die on the cross for us.

One day, Jesus walked to the Jordan River, where John preached. John and Jesus were relatives. They were part of the same family.

Show the first picture on Poster E, and point to John. **Lots and lots of people were at the Jordan River listening to John. John told them, "You are not doing what God wants you to do. Be sorry for your sins. God is sending a Savior. He will be here soon." Many people listened to John. They were sorry for their sins, and John baptized them.**

Show the second picture on the poster. **Jesus walked up to John and said, "I want you to baptize Me too."**

John was surprised. He said, "Jesus, I shouldn't baptize You! You should baptize me!" John knew that Jesus is the Son of God. Jesus did not need to be baptized.

But Jesus said, "You must do as I say because God, My Father in heaven, wants Me to be baptized." Jesus knew this was God's will. His Baptism would show people that He is God's Son. It would also begin the time when Jesus would go and tell the people that He is the Savior. So John and Jesus went into the water together, and John baptized Jesus.

Show the third picture on the poster. **As Jesus came out of the water, something wonderful happened. God the Holy Spirit came from heaven. He looked like a dove and came to sit on Jesus. Then God the Father spoke from heaven. He said, "This is My Son, whom I love. I am pleased with Him." This is how God showed that Jesus is His Son. Now Jesus was ready to begin His work of saving people from their sins.**

God calls us by our names too. He makes us His children in Holy Baptism and washes away our sins for Jesus' sake. Now, we belong to Him and are part of His family, the Church. Someday we will live with Him in heaven forever.

Bible Story Review

What you do: Hand out Lesson Leaflet 11, stickers, and crayons. Show the picture on Lesson Leaflet 11. Ask these questions to review.

Ask **What is Jesus doing in the water?** John is baptizing Him.

Where does the dove come from? Heaven; it is the Holy Spirit.

What does the voice say? This is My Son, whom I love. I am pleased with Him.

Growing in CHRiST

Direct attention to the sidebar pictures. Give children stickers to put on the dove and Jesus. Then have children find Jesus and the dove in the Bible story picture. Tell them to use their fingers to trace a line between the sets of pictures.

Ask **Who spoke from heaven? What did God say?** (You are My beloved Son.) Give children a sticker of what God said to put on the picture. Then have children connect the dots on the shell. **What did you make?** (A shell)

Say **Shells remind us of Baptism, when God calls us by name and makes us His children. Turn the page over. Look for other things that remind you of Baptism, and color them.**

Option: Review the story, using this action poem with the children.

Say **Jesus walked down to the river**—*Walk in place.*
The Savior God had sent. *Point up.*
John the Baptizer met Him; *Walk in place.*
Into the water they went. *Use arms as if wading.*
John baptized the Savior. *Pretend to pour water.*
God's Spirit came down from above. *Flutter hands.*
As Jesus walked out of the water. *Walk in place.*
God said, "See, My Son, whom I love." *Cup hand behind ear.*

(Adapted from *Fingers Tell the Story*, p. 59)

Bible Words

What you do: Have the children join you in the opening rhyme and say the Bible Words with you as you read Isaiah 43:1: "I have called you by name, you are Mine."

Ask **What did God say when He spoke from heaven?** Accept answers.

Say **Yes, God said Jesus is His Son. God wanted everyone to know that He had sent His Son, Jesus, to begin His special work of being our Savior.**

Our Bible Words tell us that God calls us by name too. He does that in Baptism and through His Word when He makes us His children by faith.

Use this Bible rhyme from *Wiggle & Wonder* (p. 28) to introduce the Bible Words.

Say **Here is the Bible God gave me.** *Open hands like book.*
What does He tell me? Let's look and see. *Shade eyes with hand.*
[God's says,] *Open Bible and read.*
"I have called you by name, *Point to children.*
you are Mine." *Point to children again.*

Say the verse together. Divide the children into two groups to learn the words.

Group 1: I have called you by name,

Group 2: you are Mine.

3 We Live (15 minutes)

Use these activities to help the children grow in their understanding of what the Bible story means for their lives. Choose the ones that work best with your class.

Growing through God's Word

What you do: Have Sprout come in singing "I Was Baptized" (*LOSP*, p. 97; CD 12).

Sprout: Hi, Teacher. I'm glad I was baptized 'cuz I'm glad to be God's child. But I've been wondering something. I know that God makes us His children when we are baptized. But what about my friend Ivy? She hasn't been baptized yet. Is she still God's child?

Teacher: Does Ivy believe in Jesus and know that He loves her?

Sprout: Oh yes! She heard about Jesus in Sunday School, and she knows He died on the cross to pay for her sins.

Teacher: Then Ivy is God's child too, because she heard God's Word and believes in Jesus.

Sprout: Oh good . . . but then why does God want us to be baptized?

Teacher: God wants everyone to be saved and be part of His family, the Church. But everyone sins. We think and say and do wrong things. And our sins keep us away from God.

Sprout: So what does Baptism do for us?

Teacher: When we are baptized or hear God's Word and believe that Jesus is our Savior, God forgives our sins. In Baptism, He puts His name on us and says we belong to Him. He makes us His children, part of His Church family. He also promises that we will go to heaven to live with Him someday.

Sprout: I'm glad I am baptized. I'm glad I'm God's child. (*Hanging head*) But sometimes, I don't act like I belong to God. Sometimes, I still do mean things. Yesterday, I hit Lily and made her cry.

Teacher: Oh, Sprout, I hope you said you were sorry.

Sprout: Yep, I did. I felt bad after I hit her. My mom knew I was sorry. She told me to remember that I was God's child. He would forgive me for hitting Lily and help me say "sorry" to her. So I told Jesus and Lily that I was sorry. Lily told me that she forgave me. I'm so happy! We're going to play together this afternoon again!

Teacher: I'm glad that you asked Lily to forgive you, Sprout. And God helped Lily to forgive you. He forgives all our sins in Baptism, and He gives us His Holy Spirit to help us live as His children. Every day, we can remember we are baptized. We can thank God for making us His children and ask Him to help us show love and forgiveness to others.

Sprout: Knowing that God loves me and that I belong to Him makes me want to jump for joy! Maybe we can sing our Baptism song and then jump for joy together? (*Do so.*)

Sing "I Was Baptized" (*LOSP*, p. 97; CD 12)

Craft Time

What you do: Give children Craft Page 11, crayons, and art supplies (tissue paper, cotton balls, snippets of wrapping paper, real or paper seashells), yarn, and stickers of shells, a cross, and Jesus with children from the Sticker Page.

Say Today, you will make a tag to show that you belong to Jesus. On one side, it says, "I belong to Jesus!" On the other side, there is a line for you to write your name. Then your tag will say, "[Emma] is a child of God." "[Nicholas] is a child of God." Name all the children. **We belong to Jesus because God made us His children through His Word and in Baptism.**

Let the children glue items onto the tag and color it. Have them add stickers of Jesus and a cross to the side that says, "I belong to Jesus." Have them add shell stickers (or real or paper seashells) to the other side. Cut out the tags; help as needed. String tags with a piece of yarn for the children to wear as necklaces.

Paper Plus option: Color and cut out the figures on Activity Page 11B. You will also need a craft stick and paper cup for each child. Follow directions on the page to make storytelling figures.

Snack Time

What you do: Mix powered lemonade with water. Tell the children that you are making something to drink that is water and something else. As you mix it, remind them that in Baptism God uses ordinary water and something else that is special—His Word—to wash away our sins and make us His children. Enjoy the lemonade together. Serve a snack of your choosing with it.

Live It Out

What you do: Make Baptism banners to hang at home as a reminder that God calls us by name through water and His Word and makes us His children. Copy Activity Page 11C for each child. Help the children write their names on the line. Give them pieces of tissue paper and ribbon to glue their pages and stickers of a baptismal font and Bible from the Sticker Page to add to the banner. Punch two holes in the top and tie with yarn to make a banner.

Encourage children to find out more about their baptismal day. When were they baptized? Where? What happened? Who was there? Who are their sponsors? Suggest they send a note to sponsors to thank them for their love and prayers.

 **4 Closing** (5 minutes)

Going Home

What you do: Send take-home pages and crafts home with the children.

Sing   "Go, My Children, with My Blessing" (*LSB* 922: CD 1) or "I Was Baptized" (*LOSP*, p. 97; CD 12) again

Say   **Remember, God makes you His child in Baptism. You belong to Jesus! Let's say this together: God makes me His child in Baptism.** Do so.

Pray   **Dear Father in heaven, thank You for sending Your Son, Jesus, to be our Savior. Thank You for making us Your children in Baptism. Help us remember every day that we belong to You! Amen.**

Reflection

What activities seemed to connect best with the children to help them understand that God makes us His children in Baptism? Pray for the children in your class this week that they might grow strong in God's Word, washed clean in their Baptism daily.

Families celebrate together. Find the hidden shells. What special celebration do shells remind you of?

Storytelling Figures

Directions: Copy, color, and cut out the figures. Glue Jesus and John to paper cups. Glue the dove to the top of a craft stick. Poke the other end of the stick through the bottom of the Jesus cup. Keep the dove below the rim of the cup. Push it up when you talk about the Holy Spirit in the shape of a dove coming to sit on Jesus.

107

God chose

_____

(name)

to be His child.

Preparing the Lesson

The Temptation of Jesus
Luke 4:1–13

Key Point

The devil tempted Jesus to sin, but Jesus, true God and true man, did not sin. He kept God's Law on our behalf and became the sinless sacrifice for our sins so that we might have forgiveness and new life.

Law/Gospel

The devil tempts me, and I often give in. **In Christ, God forgives my sin, provides all that I need for this life and the next, and gives me power to overcome temptation.**

Context

This event occurs immediately after Jesus' Baptism and marks the beginning of His ministry. Exhausted after fasting for forty days, Jesus engages Satan in spiritual combat, overcoming every temptation by the power of God's Word.

Commentary

In this account, Jesus is "full of the Holy Spirit," having just been baptized (3:21–22). The Holy Spirit leads our Savior not to glory but to suffering. Jesus goes about His saving work through His active obedience. The glory will follow. Jesus is in the desert, the place of sterility and chaos, as opposed to Paradise, the place of fertility and order (Genesis 2). Jesus is there for forty days. This recalls the wanderings of Israel in the desert for forty years (Deuteronomy 8:2) and Moses on Mt. Sinai for forty days (Exodus 24:18).

Jesus is tempted by the devil. The Greek word *diabolos* ("devil," cf. Spanish *diablo*) means "slanderer" or "accuser." The devil always accuses us before the judgment seat of God. But Christ is our advocate who pleads for us, offering His own blood in expiation of our guilt. This passage contrasts Adam with Christ, who is the last Adam. Adam began in Paradise, was tempted, fell, and went from life to death. Jesus began in the desert, was tempted but overcame, and went from death to life.

There are three temptations. Each centers on and challenges the identity of Jesus—which Satan well knows—as the Son of God. Luke has established that Jesus is the Son of God in his accounts of the Baptism (3:22) and the genealogy (3:38), which precede this passage. To each temptation, Jesus responds with the written Word of God, all quotes from Deuteronomy.

Jesus is hungry after fasting for forty days. Satan tempts Him not only to feed Himself but also to become a bread king, appealing to man's most base desires. Jesus cites Deuteronomy 8:3: "Man does not live by bread alone." Matthew adds that we live spiritually by the Word of God. Having overcome this temptation, Jesus is qualified to feed men's bodies with bread, as in the feeding of the five thousand, and to feed their souls with the bread of life in Holy Communion (Matthew 26:26).

Next, Satan claims to have authority over the kingdoms of this world, and he will give those kingdoms to Jesus if Jesus worships him. Satan is lying. He is king only over sinners and not a complete ruler even at that. We soon see in Luke that Jesus has true divine authority in His teaching (4:32) and in His miracles (4:36). Jesus counters by citing Deuteronomy 6:13: "You shall worship the Lord your God, and Him only shall you serve" (Luke 4:8). Jesus is, of course, the Second Person of the Holy Trinity and Himself worthy of worship. Indeed, at the name of Jesus every knee shall bow (Philippians 2:10), including the devil's.

Satan in the last temptation quotes, or rather misquotes, Scripture, citing Psalm 91:11–12. Seeing that the devil can twist Scripture, we cannot be too careful about pure doctrine. The devil here, as in all temptations, wants Jesus—and us in our Christian life—to bypass the cross and go straight to the glory. But Jesus quotes Deuteronomy 6:16 and defeats the devil by telling him not to tempt God. Jesus Christ Himself is God—God who suffers and dies for you and me.

To hear an in-depth discussion of this Bible account, visit cph.org/podcast and listen to our Seeds of Faith podcast each week.

Lesson 12

The Temptation of Jesus

Luke 4:1–13

Connections

Bible Words
[Jesus said,] "I am the way, and the truth, and the life." John 14:6 (CD 6)

Faith Word
Tempt

Hymn
Go, My Children, with My Blessing (*LSB* 922; CD 1)

Catechism
Lord's Prayer: Sixth and Seventh Petitions

Take-Home Point
Jesus won the victory over sin and the devil for me.

 1 Opening (15 minutes)

Welcome Time

What you do: Set up two activity areas. In one, set out copies of Activity Page 12A, a Jesus sticker, and crayons. For added interest, supply wide satin ribbon, scissors, sequins, and the like. Have children cut out their completed prize ribbon and attach additional satin ribbon streamers to it. In the other area, clear enough space to play a game of Simon Says. Make copies of Activity Page Fun (below and on CD) for parents or a classroom helper. Adjust talk as necessary.

Play the CD from your Teacher Tools. Greet the children, give them a sticker to put on the attendance chart, and have them put their offering in the basket.

Say Hi, [Lila]. I'm glad you are here! Today, we're going to hear about the time Jesus said no to the devil! Help the child find a friend and get started in an activity.

Activity Page Fun Get a copy of Activity Page 12A and a Jesus sticker. Show the Activity Page to your child.

Ask Do you know what this is? It's a ribbon that someone might win in a contest or race for coming in first or doing the best job. Help your child understand what it is and why he or she might win a ribbon.

Today, you will hear how Jesus won against the tricky devil. The devil wanted Jesus to do what he said, instead of what God says. We call the devil's tricks and traps *temptations*. But Jesus always obeyed God and didn't sin. He won against the devil. He did that for us. That makes us winners too. Have the children color their ribbon and add a sticker of Jesus to it to show that they are winners through Jesus' victory on the cross.

MATERIALS NEEDED

1 Opening	2 God Speaks	3 We Live	4 Closing
Teacher Tools Attendance chart & CD	**Teacher Tools** CD	**Student Pack** Craft Page 12 Stickers	**Teacher Tools** CD
Student Pack Attendance sticker Jesus sticker	**Student Pack** Lesson Leaflet 12	**Other Supplies** Sprout & toy Graham crackers & tube frosting Ribbon or fabric, string, cups (optional) Paper Plus supplies (optional)	**Student Pack** Take-home materials
Other Supplies Activity Page 12A (TG) Resource Page 1 (TG) Wide satin ribbon, sequins (optional)	**Other Supplies** Activity Page 12B Sprout or another puppet Toy for Sprout *The Story of Jesus' Baptism and Temptation* Arch Book (optional)		

Active Learning Play Simon Says. Talk about how it is easy to get tricked and do things other than what Simon tells us to do.

Say In today's story, the devil tries to trick Jesus to do what he says rather than what God says. We call the devil's tricks and traps *temptations*.

Sing a cleanup song (Resource Page 1) to cue the children to clean up. Help them put away the materials; then use the following rhyme to gather them for your opening.

Say Come and learn of Jesus, our Savior and our Friend.
Come and worship Jesus; His love is without end.

Gathering in God's Name

What you do: Begin with this opening. To teach about the Church Year, use the materials in the Church Year Worship Kit.

Sing "Our Church Family" (*LOSP*, p. 11; CD 15) or another opening song

Invite the children to say the Invocation and Amen with you. Tell them "Amen" is the special word they get to say at the end of prayers, hymns, and parts of the church service.

Begin In the name of the Father and of the Son and of the Holy Spirit. Amen.

Offering Have a child bring the offering basket forward. Sing an offering song.

Pray Dear Father, thank You for sending Jesus to be our Savior. Help us to listen as we learn about You from the Bible. Amen.

Celebrate Birthdays, Baptism birthdays, and special occasions

2 God Speaks (20 minutes)

Story Clue

What you do: Put a small car or other toy in Sprout's backpack with a corner of it sticking out. *Option:* Create a puppet show of this dialogue, using the "Sock Puppets" app available for iPhone, Ipod touch, or iPad.

Teacher: Hi, Sprout. (*Spying toy*) Did you bring a new [car] to show us?

Sprout: (*Acting guilty*) No . . . it isn't new. *Actually* it belongs to Lily. We were playing [cars] at her house the other day, and I really liked this one. So when it was time to leave, I just kinda put it in my backpack.

Teacher: Oh, I see. That toy was a temptation to you.

Sprout: A temptation? What does that mean?

Teacher: God says some things are wrong. When we want to do something that we know God says is wrong, we call that a temptation.

Sprout: (*Hangs head*) I know I shouldn't have taken it. But I wanted it so bad.

Teacher: I know, Sprout. The devil tries to trick us into doing wrong things. God doesn't want us to take things that belong to others, though. That is a sin. Do you remember Adam and Eve, the first two people God made?

Sprout: Yeah, a little. They lived in a really pretty garden with tigers and bears and lots of animals. And they all got along!

Teacher: That's right. But one day, God's enemy, the devil, came into the Garden of Eden and tricked them. He wanted Adam and Eve to listen to him instead of to God. And you know what? The devil won! Adam and Eve didn't do what God told them to do. They listened to the devil. They sinned.

Sprout: Yeah, and then they had to leave the garden. That was so sad.

Teacher: Yes, but that isn't the saddest part. Their sin brought trouble and sadness and sickness and death into the world. Now, all people sin. All people get sick and have troubles. But there is a happy part to the story too. God made a plan to save Adam and Eve and all people.

Sprout: (*Interrupting*) I know. I know. He sent Jesus!

Teacher: Yes, God sent His Son, Jesus, to be the Savior of the world! To save us, Jesus had to keep God's Law and never sin. Then He had to pay for our sins on the cross. In today's story, Jesus is in a desert. And guess who comes to try to tempt Jesus to sin?

Sprout: Oh, no! Not that tricky devil again.

Teacher: (*Nod head yes.*) Yes, God's enemy, the devil! He wants to mess up God's plan again. So he tries to trick Jesus to listen to him instead of God. Let's listen to our Bible story and find out who wins this time!

Bible Story Time

What you do: You need the CD and Activity Page 12B. Enlarge and photo-copy the pictures. Color them, cut them apart, and mount them on construction paper. Fold back the sections with the bread, crown, and angel so they don't show. Reveal them when you talk about each of the devil's temptations.

Draw a cross over each temptation when you say that Jesus won and the devil lost. Listen to the story on track 20 of the CD or tell it using the teacher talk here.

Say **At Jesus' Baptism, God spoke from heaven and said, "You are My beloved Son." Then the Holy Spirit sent Jesus into the desert for forty days and forty nights. Jesus prayed and did not eat. He was very hungry.** Show Jesus in desert. **God's enemy, the devil, came to tempt Jesus. He tried to trick Jesus into doing something bad. The devil knew that Jesus was hungry. He said, "Turn these stones into bread."** Unfold the section to reveal the bread.

But Jesus saw the trap. He didn't fall for the devil's trick. Jesus used God's Word to answer the devil. Jesus said, "We need God's Word more than we need bread." Jesus could have turned the stones into bread very easily. But He didn't do what the devil told Him to do. Jesus was tempted, but He did not sin. Jesus won, and the devil lost. Draw a cross over the bread.

Next, God's enemy, the devil, took Jesus to a very high place. He showed Jesus all the kingdoms of the world. Show picture of Jesus and distant city. **Then the devil told Jesus, "I will give this to You. You can be king over all of it if You just fall down and worship me."** Unfold the section to reveal crown.

But Jesus saw the trap. He didn't fall for the devil's trick. Jesus used God's Word to answer the devil. Jesus said, "God's Word says that we should worship only God." Jesus knew that it would be very wrong to

Key Point

The devil tempted Jesus to sin, but Jesus, true God and true man, did not sin. He kept God's Law on our behalf and became the sinless sacrifice for our sins so that we might have forgiveness and new life.

worship God's enemy. He knew that God says we are to worship only Him. Jesus was tempted, but He did not sin. Jesus won, and the devil lost. Draw a cross over the crown.

But God's enemy, the devil, didn't give up. He tried to trick Jesus one more time. He took Jesus to a high place on the temple. Show the picture of Jesus on the temple roof. Then the devil told Jesus, "If You are the Son of God, jump down. You don't have to be afraid. God's angels will keep You safe. It says so in the Bible." Unfold the section to reveal an angel.

But Jesus saw the trap. He didn't fall for the devil's trick. Jesus used God's Word to answer the devil. Jesus said, "God's Word says that we should not test God." Jesus knew that the devil was trying to make Him show that He was the Son of God. Jesus knew that He didn't have to prove anything to the devil! Jesus was tempted, but He did not sin. Jesus won, and the devil lost. Draw a cross over the angel. Then the devil left, and angels came to take care of Jesus.

God's enemy, the devil, tempts us to sin too. He tries to trap us into disobeying what God says in His Word. Lots of times, we do fall for the devil's tricks—we sin. But Jesus is God's Son. He is stronger than the devil. When the devil tempted Jesus, Jesus never sinned. He did everything right. Turn the page over and draw a large cross on it. Then He was punished for our sins on the cross. Because of Jesus, our story has a happy ending. Because of Jesus, God forgives our sins. Because of Jesus, we will live forever with God in a beautiful place called heaven!

Bible Story Review

What you do: Hand out Lesson Leaflet 12 and crayons. Point to the Bible story picture as you review with the questions.

Option: Use *The Story of Jesus' Baptism and Temptation* Arch Book (CPH, 59-1503) to review these events in our Savior's life.

Ask **Where is Jesus?** On the roof of the temple.

What does the devil want Jesus to do? Jump off.

What does Jesus use when He answers the devil? God's Word.

Direct children to the activity on side 1 of the leaflet. Ask the children to place a finger on each of the pictures in the sidebar as you say the word describing the picture. Read from top to bottom.

Ask **What did Jesus use to say no to the devil?**

Have the children circle the correct picture. On side 2, have the children connect the dots on the Bible. Talk about how God works through His Word to strengthen our faith in Him and to forgive our sins.

Bible Words

What you do: Read the Bible Words from John 14:6. Say the verse and then play it on track 6 of the CD, or use the action song to help the children learn the words.

Say Every Sunday, we learn words from God's Word, the Bible. In the Bible, Jesus tells us (read from Bible), **"I am the way, and the truth, and the life."** Let's say that together. Do so.

Jesus is the one true way to heaven. He won the victory over the devil. He said no to the devil's tricks, and He didn't sin; He died on the cross to pay for our sins. Jesus is our Savior. He makes us winners and gives us life with Him forever.

Play the Bible words on the CD, and encourage the children to join in. *Option:* Have children line up in a row, one behind the other. You and a helper (or another child) hold your arms together like a drawbridge. Tell children to walk under the drawbridge. As they do, sing the song to the tune of "London Bridge." As each child walks forward, lower the bridge (your arms) and "catch" the child inside your arms. Help the child say the Bible Words to get out of the gate.

Sing **Heaven's gate is open wide, open wide, open wide.**
Hold arms up, like a drawbridge, so child can walk under them.
Heaven's gate is open wide; come meet Jesus.
Jesus loves you; yes, He does; Yes, He does; yes, He does.
Jesus loves you; yes, He does. He's our Savior.
Lower arms around child.

Ask What did Jesus say? Help child say the Bible Words: **[Jesus said,] "I am the way, and the truth, and the life."**

③ We Live (15 minutes)

Use these activities to help the children grow in their understanding of what the Bible story means for them. Choose the ones that work best with your class.

Growing through God's Word

What you do: Have Sprout come in with the toy.

Teacher: What's the problem, Sprout? You don't look too happy.

Sprout: (*Looking at toy*) Oh, I just feel bad that I took Lily's [car].

Teacher: That's because taking things that don't belong to you is a sin. We should feel bad about the wrong things we think and say and do. But we can ask God to forgive us because of Jesus. We can ask God to make us strong against sin too. In the Lord's Prayer, we pray, "And lead us not into temptation." When we pray that, we are asking God to help us so we don't do things that get us or others into trouble. We are asking Him to help us fight against sin.

Sprout: How do you fight sin? Do you kick or punch it? (*Sprout punches airs.*)

Teacher: No, we can't punch or kick sin. But God gives us something better. It's His Word. God helps our faith grow strong through His Word and Baptism. He tells us what He wants us to do and not do in His Word. When we listen to His Word, He helps us say no to sin.

Sprout: (*Looking at toy again*) Yeah, but it's hard. Even when I try to be good, I still mess up. I don't always say no to sin.

Growing in CHRIST

Teacher: I know, Sprout. Even when we believe in Jesus, we are still weak and sinful. But Jesus is strong. He won the victory *for us* over sin, death, and the devil. Because of Jesus, God forgives us. He keeps on helping us get stronger through His Word. And someday He will take us to live with Him in heaven.

Sprout: That's good news! I think I'll go give Lily her car back!

Craft Time

What you do: Use Craft Page 12, stickers, and crayons to make a cross. *Option:* Cut purple ribbon to glue to the robe and pieces of string to glue to the rope. Tape the cross to an upside-down paper cup.

Say   **We are going to make a cross to remind us that the devil lost when Jesus died on the cross to pay for our sins. Because Jesus did that, God forgives our sins and gives us life with Him in heaven.**

Have children color the rocky ground and add rock stickers. Give them a crown of thorns to add to the cross. Have them color the robe purple. Talk about how Jesus wore a purple robe and crown of thorns before He died on the cross for us. Cut out the cross and tape the base in a circle to make the cross stand up, or tape it around a paper cup for added stability.

Paper Plus option: Hand out copies of Activity Page 12B. Discuss the pictures, and have students draw crosses over the bread, crown, and angel to remind them that Jesus is our Savior. Have them add Bible stickers to show that Jesus used God's Word to resist the devil. Glue the page to construction paper; then cut apart the scenes. Assemble them in order; staple on side to make a booklet of the story.

Snack Time

What you do: Use tubes of frosting to make crosses on graham crackers to look like Bibles.

Live It Out

Encourage children to use their craft or Paper Plus activity to tell someone the Bible story and how Jesus won the victory over sin, death, and the devil for us.

4 Closing (5 minutes)

Going Home

What you do: Send take-home pages and crafts with the children.

Sing   "Go, My Children, with My Blessing" (*LSB* 922; CD 1) or "Ponder and Praise" (*S&W*, p. 24)

Say   **When Jesus said no to the devil, He kept God's Law for us. Then He paid for our sins on the cross. Let's say, "Jesus won the victory over sin and the devil for me" together.** Do so.

Pray   **Dear Jesus, thank You for beating the devil for us! Help us say no to sin too, and forgive us for all the times we don't. Amen.**

Reflection

Did you reassure the children that Jesus loves them and forgives them always?

[Jesus said,] "I am the way, and the truth, and the life." John 14:6
Jesus won the victory over sin and the devil. He gives eternal life.

Preparing the Lesson

Jesus Calls Philip and Nathanael

John 1:43–51

Date of Use

Key Point

Jesus called Philip and Nathanael to believe in Him. In Jesus, access to heaven is given to all who believe.

Law/**Gospel**

My sinful nature does not recognize Jesus as the Son of God. I futilely try to manipulate Jesus into being what I want. **Jesus is the only true God, the Savior who rescues me from sin, death, and the devil. He is the true Jacob's ladder upon whom the angels will come down and escort me to my heavenly home.**

Context

There is a changeover between John the Baptist and Jesus. Before Jesus is baptized, and even long after, John has his disciples while Jesus has His (Matthew 9:14; John 1:35; 4:1; Acts 19:1–7).

Only over time did the two groups become one. One of the Baptist's followers, Andrew, has already come to follow Jesus, bringing his brother Simon Peter with him. Here, Philip and Nathanael (also known as Bartholomew) confess faith in the Savior—Nathanael a tad reluctantly at first.

Right after this account of Jesus calling Philip and Nathanael in John's Gospel, we have the wedding at Cana. In it, we see something of a "parable" of the transition from John the Baptist to Jesus when water (John) is transformed into wine (Messiah).

Commentary

Philip recognizes Jesus from His Old Testament prebiography. As Philip tells Nathanael, "We have found Him of whom Moses in the Law and also the prophets wrote, Jesus of Nazareth, the son of Joseph" (John 1:45). Moses wrote of Jesus? Yes, as did all the Old Testament prophets (e.g., Luke 24:25–27, 44; John 5:39, 46; Acts 3:18–24).

The Messiah is the be-all and end-all of the Bible, from Genesis through Revelation. Foretold in prophecy and fore-shadowed in various Old Testament individuals, objects, and actions, He was as much the Savior for Old Testament sinners as He is for us.

Nathanael, while believing in the Messiah, did not expect Him to come from Nazareth. Perhaps from Bethlehem or Jerusalem, but not Nazareth! Ah, yes, but Jesus, while He may not fit Nathanael's preconceived ideas about where the Messiah should come from, shows that He is, indeed, the Messiah.

He knows all. Seeing Nathanael, Jesus pronounces him "an Israelite indeed, in whom there is no deceit!" (John 1:47), the one Jesus knew was "under the fig tree" (v. 48) without actually seeing him there. This judgment of Nathanael's character, as well as his exact location, astounds Nathanael into confessing the divinity and royalty of Jesus.

But once again, Jesus bursts out of the limiting bonds we set for Him. He tells Nathanael that he will see greater things than Jesus' omniscience. He will see "heaven opened, and the angels of God ascending and descending on the Son of Man" (v. 51). The allusion here is to Jacob's ladder (Genesis 28:10–22), on which the angels went up and down, as seen in Jacob's dream at Bethel.

What Nathanael will see is that in Jesus, access to heaven is given to all who believe. Those celestial messengers will escort us to heaven on the basis of Jesus' life, death, and resurrection. On the stairsteps of His flesh, we shall ascend to the true Bethel ("house of God") above.

To hear an in-depth discussion of this Bible account, visit cph.org/podcast and listen to our Seeds of Faith podcast each week.

Preparing the Lesson © 2008, 2015 Concordia Publishing House. Scripture: ESV®.

Jesus Calls Philip and Nathanael

John 1:43–51

Connections

Bible Words
[Jesus says,] "Follow Me."
John 1:43

Faith Word
Disciple

Hymn
Go, My Children, with My Blessing (*LSB* 922; CD 1)

Catechism
Apostles' Creed:
Third Article

Holy Baptism

Liturgy
Holy Baptism

Take-Home Point
Jesus is the way to heaven.

 1 Opening (15 minutes)

Welcome Time

What you do: Set up two activity areas. In one, set out copies of Activity Page 13 and crayons. In the other area, set out puzzles or blocks. Make copies of Activity Page Fun (below and on CD) for parents or a classroom helper. Adjust talk as necessary.

Play the CD from your Teacher Tools. Greet the children, give them a sticker to put on the attendance chart, and have them put their offering in the basket.

Say Hi, [Quinn]. How are you? I wonder . . . what are some things you like to do with your friends? Help the child find a friend and get started in an activity.

Activity Page Fun Get a copy of the Activity Page and crayons. Show the page to your child.

Ask Who is this? (Jesus) Read the Bible Words. **Can you draw yourself with Jesus? Today, you will hear how Jesus called two people to follow Him and be His friends. Listen to the Bible story. You can tell it to me after Sunday School.**

MATERIALS NEEDED

1 Opening	2 God Speaks	3 We Live	4 Closing
Teacher Tools Attendance chart & CD	**Teacher Tools** CD Poster F	**Student Pack** Craft Page 13 Stickers	**Teacher Tools** CD
Student Pack Attendance sticker	**Student Pack** Lesson Leaflet 13	**Other Supplies** Baby scrapbook, pictures, or items Finger Jell-O children	**Student Pack** Take-home items
Other Supplies Activity Page 13 (TG) Puzzles or blocks Resource Page 1 (TG)	**Other Supplies** Sprout or another puppet Toy phone *The Twelve Ordinary Men* Arch Book (optional)	Fish for food Paper Plus supplies (optional) Craft sticks (optional)	

Active Learning Set out puzzles or blocks. Have the children work together.

Say It is nice to have friends to work and play with. Jesus is our best friend. He loves us and came to be our Savior. Today, you will hear how Jesus asked a man named Philip to follow Him and learn more about God's love. Philip went and told his friend about Jesus. Philip wanted his friend to know Jesus was their Savior and to follow Him too.

Use your classroom cleanup signal, and then gather for circle time. Do an action poem from Resource Page 1 to get the wiggles out.

Gathering in God's Name

What you do: Gather the children, and begin with this opening. To teach about the Church Year, use the materials in the Church Year Worship Kit.

Sing "Our Church Family" (*LOSP*, p. 11; CD 15)

Invite the children to say the Invocation and Amen with you. Tell them "Amen" is the special word they get to say at the end of prayers, hymns, and parts of the church service.

Begin In the name of the Father and of the Son and of the Holy Spirit. Amen.

Offering Have a child bring the offering basket forward. Sing an offering song.

Celebrate Birthdays, Baptism birthdays, and special occasions

Pray Repeat after me. Have children echo your words after the asterisks. **Dear God,* thank You for a new day.* Thank You for church.* Thank You for calling us* through Baptism and Your Word* to be Your children.* Amen.***

Celebrate Birthdays, Baptism birthdays, and special occasions

② God Speaks (20 minutes)

Story Clue

What you do: Use Sprout or another puppet.

Sprout: Hi, everybody! (*Sprout waves to children.*) It's so nice to see all of my friends here today! I like having lots of friends. Friends are special!

Teacher: Hi, Sprout. Friends *are* special! What do you do with your friends?

Sprout: Um, I like to play and build roads together. My cousin Lily helps me put together Legos sets. They're hard for me, but Lily makes cool things. (*Turns to children.*) What do you like to do with your friends? (*Accepts ideas.*)

Teacher: It is a lot of fun to have friends. They are a gift from God! The Bible tells us that Jesus had friends too.

Sprout: I wonder what Jesus and His friends did together . . .

Teacher: I don't know, Sprout. The Bible doesn't tell us everything, but it does tell us that Jesus chose some men to follow Him. We call these men the disciples. Today, we're going to hear about the time Jesus called two of His disciples. Would you like to stay and listen, Sprout? (*Sprout nods yes.*)

Bible Story Time

What you do: Use a toy phone, a CD player, and the CD from your Teacher Tools. Play the story on the CD (track 21) when indicated below, or tell it, using the following script and Poster F. Have the children join you in the indicated motions. Play the ringer on a toy phone or your cell phone, or say "Ring, ring."

Option: Use *The Twelve Ordinary Men* Arch Book (CPH, 59-2222) to tell how Jesus called all twelve of His disciples.

Say RING, RING. That sounds like a phone, doesn't it? I wonder who is calling. Maybe it is a friend or someone who wants to tell me something important. Who else might call on the phone? Accept suggestions.

Today, we're going to hear the true story of how Jesus called two men to follow Him. We call these men disciples. Can you say *disciple* with me? Do so. *Disciple* is another word for "student." You are my students, and I am your teacher. Jesus called these men to be His students. Jesus wanted to teach the men about God's love and show them that He was the Savior God promised to send.

RING, RING! Do you think Jesus called these men on the phone? No, Jesus didn't use a phone. He walked over to the men and used His voice to call them. Let's listen to our story on the CD. Every time you hear the word *call*, use your hand to wave someone to come closer (demonstrate a beckoning motion). When you hear the word *tell*, put your hand to your mouth and pretend to whisper a secret to your friend.

Play Begin the CD story now or continue with the script.

Say When Jesus was baptized, He showed that He was God's Son. Now Jesus wanted to tell (cup hands around mouth) **many people about God's love. He wanted people to hear that He was the one God had sent to save them from their sins. Jesus could have done this work all by Himself. But instead, He went to look for some helpers. First, Jesus walked along and saw Philip. "Philip," Jesus called** (motion to come), **"Come, follow Me!"**

Philip was happy to follow Jesus. Philip wanted his friend to know about Jesus too. So, he ran to tell (cup hands around mouth) **Nathanael. Nathanael was sitting under a fig tree. "Nathanael," Philip called** (motion to come). **"Come with me! We have found the Savior. He is Jesus of Nazareth. Come and see!" So, Nathanael went with Philip to meet Jesus.**

When Jesus saw Nathanael, He said, "Here is someone who trusts in God's promises."

Nathanael was puzzled. He asked, "How do You know who I am?"

Jesus answered, "I saw you sitting under the fig tree before Philip called (beckon) **you."**

Nathanael was surprised. He said, "Teacher, You are the Son of God!"

Jesus said, "You believe I am God's Son because I said I saw you under the fig tree. But I tell (cup hands around mouth) **you that you will see many more amazing things than this."**

Philip and Nathanael left their homes and followed Jesus. Show Poster F.

Key Point

Jesus called Philip and Nathanael to believe in Him. In Jesus, access to heaven is given to all who believe.

Growing in CHRIST

They knew Jesus loved them very much. They went everywhere that Jesus went. They watched Jesus and learned from Him. They listened to Jesus tell (cup hands around mouth) **others about God's love and how He had come to save them from their sins. One day, they would tell** (cup hands around mouth) **many people how Jesus had come to be the Savior of all.**

Jesus wants everyone to know that He is the Savior. He wants everyone to believe in Him. He calls (beckon) **us to be His followers too, through Baptism and His Word. He forgives our sins and helps us share His love in what we say and do.**

Bible Story Review

What you do: Use Poster F and the questions to review the story. Then hand out Lesson Leaflet 13 and crayons.

Ask **What did Jesus tell Philip to do?** He said, "Follow Me."

Whom did Philip go tell? Nathanael

What did Philip tell Nathanael about Jesus? He said Jesus is the Savior.

Direct attention to the sidebar activity on the leaflets. Count and find the items in the Bible picture; then do the maze on side 2.

Play a review game called "Jesus Loves Us So!" Have one child pretend to be Jesus in the middle of the circle. Have the rest of the children form a circle around this child as you sing to the tune of "The Farmer in the Dell." *Note:* It's easy for children to feel left out. Tell them that *everyone* will get a turn. Find ways for children with special needs to be included too.

Sing **Jesus loves us so! Jesus loves us so!**
He calls our names; we're never the same . . . 'cause Jesus loves us so!

Say **Now we need Jesus to call Philip!** Let the child in the middle choose a child to be Philip. Have Philip join Jesus in the circle. Sing the refrain again.

Now we need Philip to call Nathanael! Let Philip choose a child to be Nathanael. Nathanael joins the circle. Sing the refrain. Continue with each child, using each child's name, until all have had a turn to be called into the circle.

Bible Words

What you do: Read John 1:43 from your Bible.

Say **The Bible tells us that Jesus gives us eternal life with God in heaven. He tells us, "Follow Me." He is the only way to get to heaven. To follow Jesus means to believe in Him. Let's say our Bible Words together.** Do so. Then play follow the leader.

Say **[Jesus says,] "Follow Me!"** Beckon children to follow you.

Lead the children to the sanctuary or around your room. Stop at a cross or Bible. Talk about how God's Word tells us Jesus is our Savior. He calls us to believe in Him and be His children. **[Jesus says,] "Follow Me!"** Lead children to another spot, such as the baptismal font, and talk about it, or pretend you have stopped there, describing what you see. Tell children that Jesus calls us through Baptism to be His children. Repeat the Bible Words. End back in your circle area. Say the Bible Words again.

Say Through Baptism and His Word, Jesus calls us to follow Him. Jesus is the way to heaven.

3 We Live (15 minutes)

Use these activities to help the children grow in their understanding of what the Bible story means for their lives. Choose the ones that work best with your class.

Growing through God's Word

What you do: Have baby pictures or baby items to show.

Talk about babies. Ask the children to share what they think they were like as babies. Did they have hair? What color? Did they cry a lot? What did they like to eat when they got older?

Say God made every person in the whole world. He knows the color of our eyes and hair. He knows our names. He knows what we like to do. He knows what we like to eat. Before we were even born, God saw us growing inside of our mommies and knew all about us. God loves us with a great big love! He loves us so much that He sent Jesus to die on the cross for us.

Jesus called Philip and Nathanael to follow Him and be His disciples. Jesus taught them about God's love. He showed them that He was the one God sent to save all people from their sins. Jesus taught them so they could go and tell others that He was the Savior.

Jesus gives us pastors, parents, teachers, and others to teach us that He is our Savior. He calls us by name in our Baptism and through His Word to be His children. He says, "Follow Me." Jesus is the way to heaven for everyone who believes in Him.

Say Jesus calls you to be His children. He helps you to share His love with others. Can you think of some ways Jesus helps you to do that?

Help children think about their calling as God's children (e.g., to obey parents, show love to family and friends, listen to teachers, invite others to church). Tell them God gives them power or help to do this. He does that through His Word and Sacraments. Assure them of God's love and forgiveness, no matter what.

Craft Time

What you do: You will need Craft Page 13, stickers, scissors, and crayons.

Cut on the horizontal line to separate the background from the puppets. Give the children a tree sticker to add to the background on side 1. Have them color the finger puppets and cut them apart. Help them cut out the finger holes. Encourage the children to tell the story to one another.

Option: Fold under or cut off the finger hole section and tape the puppets to craft sticks. Demonstrate how to use the puppets by telling the Bible story in a few words with the puppets on your fingers or by moving them on sticks.

Paper Plus option: Make a friendship prayer flower pot. For each child, push a Styrofoam ball, sized to fit, into a small clay pot. Give the children markers, craft

Growing in CHRIST.

paint, or stickers from their sticker sheets to decorate their pots. Cut out hearts or circles from poster board or craft foam to make flowers and attach them to craft sticks. Stick these into the pots.

Take digital pictures of the children. Cut around the faces on the pictures so they fit onto the craft stick flowers, and tape them in place. Talk about the gift of friends and how we can pray for our friends so that they would know Jesus as their Savior.

Snack Time

What you do: Make finger Jell-O, and cut it into boy and girl shapes. Talk about friends and how Jesus is our best friend and Savior. He called Philip to follow Him. Philip told his friend Nathanael. Jesus calls us to follow Him. He helps us share His love with our friends and others too.

Live It Out

Collect fish food. Ask children to bring canned tuna, salmon, crab, pickled herring, and the like, to donate to your church or community food pantry. Talk about how most of Jesus' disciples were fishermen. He called them to follow Him and learn from Him so they could tell others that He is the Savior God promised to send. Jesus calls us to follow Him too. He helps us to show love for others by caring for their needs.

4 Closing (5 minutes)

Going Home

Sing "Go, My Children, with My Blessing" (*LSB* 922; CD 1) or "Ponder and Praise" (*S&W*, p. 24)

Say Jesus says, "Follow Me." He is the way to heaven. Let's say, "Jesus is the way to heaven" together. Repeat point. **Jesus calls us to be His children through Baptism and His Word. He forgives us and helps us share His love in what we say and do.**

Pray **Dear God, You love us so much! Thank You for calling us to follow You. Help us to share Your love with others. In Your name we pray. Amen.**

Reflection

Think about how the children are growing in their abilities and skills. What kinds of things are they more capable of doing now than even a month ago? Consider activities and projects that allow them to use their new abilities.

[Jesus says,] "Follow Me!" John 1:43

Songs & Wiggles-Out Rhymes

Young children must use their large muscles and move around in order to process and learn new information. Incorporate music and movement between periods of quieter learning to allow for this. Give children scarves or ribbon twirlers to use as they sing.

Songs

Cleanup Song 1
Tune: "Row, Row, Row Your Boat"

Clean, clean, clean the room.
Put our things away.
Help, help, help, help—
Then we'll sing and pray.

Cleanup Song 2
Tune: "London Bridge"

Clean up, clean up, everyone,
Everywhere, everywhere.
Clean up, clean up, everyone.
Come, do your share.

Gathering Song
Tune: "Mary Had a Little Lamb"

Come and listen to God's Word,
To God's Word, to God's Word.
Come and listen to God's Word
From His book, the Bible.

Welcome Song
Tune: "Do, Lord!"

Welcome, we welcome, we welcome you today.
Welcome, we welcome, we welcome you today.
Welcome, we welcome, we welcome you today.
It's time to sing and pray.

Birthday Song
Tune: "London Bridge"

We're so glad that you were born,
You were born, you were born.
We're so glad that you were born,
Thank You, Jesus

Baptism Song
Tune: "Mary Had a Little Lamb"

God chose [child's name] to be His child,
Be His child, Be His child.
God chose [child's name] to be His child,
Through Baptism and His Word.

Snack Song
Tune: "London Bridge Is Falling Down"

Thank You, God, for food and drink,
Food and drink, food and drink.
Thank You, God, for food and drink.
How You love us!

Wiggles-Out Rhymes

Wiggles Out 1

Stretch up high.
Stretch down low.
Swing your arms to and fro.
Clap your hands, 1, 2, 3.
Then sit as quietly as can be.
Use actions to accompany the words.

Wiggles Out 2

Clap your hands for Jesus, 1, 2, 3.
He loves you, and He loves me.
Stomp your feet for Jesus; He's our King.
He can protect us from anything!
Wave your arms for Jesus, to and fro.
He is with us wherever we go!
Hooray! *Clap and cheer.*

Wiggles Out 3

Clap your hands and shout, "Hooray!"
We will learn of God today.
Stomp your feet and say, "Amen."
Jesus is our special friend.
Lean to the left; lean to the right.
Clap for God with all your might.

Wait, Wait, Wait, Go

Have children stand still.
Slowly say, "Wait, wait, wait."
When you say, "Go," tell them they can wiggle, jump, and move around until you say, "Stop." Repeat. Talk about waiting.

Getting Ready to Pray

Ten little fingers ready to play. *Wiggle fingers.*
Ten little fingers ready to pray. *Fold hands.*
Help me, dear Jesus, in every way *Bow head.*
To love and serve You every day. *Extend hands.*

Introducing the Bible Words

Here is the Bible God gave to me.
Open hands like book.

What does He tell me? Let's look and see.
Shade eyes with hand.

From *Wiggle & Wonder*, p. 28 © 2012 CPH.

Supply List

Every Week

Have a Bible, catechism, hymnal, children's songbook, offering basket, puppet, and CD player for use every week, as well as classroom supplies such as scissors, tape, glue, construction paper, stapler, hole punch, yarn or ribbon, and crayons or markers.

Other Supplies

Many of these supplies are for Welcome Time or optional crafts. See each lesson to choose what you want to do; then highlight the supplies you'll need. Paper Plus supplies are listed within the lesson.

Lesson 1

- ❏ Paper bags
- ❏ Baby items & angel
- ❏ Paper cups
- ❏ Angel sugar cookies
- ❏ Ribbon or crepe paper

Optional
- ❏ Play dough & craft sticks
- ❏ Incense or a candle
- ❏ Garland or bathrobe
- ❏ Ribbon or crepe paper

Lesson 2

- ❏ Play dough & cookie cutters
- ❏ Envelope & letter
- ❏ Baby picture
- ❏ Bookmark or other gift
- ❏ Sugar cookies & tube frosting

Optional
- ❏ Pictures of angels & Jesus
- ❏ Decorating supplies
- ❏ *Mary's Christmas Story* Arch Book
- ❏ Garland & towel

Lesson 3

- ❏ Wrapping-paper, bows, gift bags & ribbon
- ❏ Blocks or boxes
- ❏ Rhythm instruments or homemade bells
- ❏ Hole punch, yarn, or ribbon
- ❏ Bugle-shaped snack chips

Optional
- ❏ Decorating supplies

Lesson 4

- ❏ Dolls & baby items
- ❏ Story bag & Christmas items
- ❏ Church directory, Bible, shell & Communion wafers
- ❏ Graham crackers, cream cheese & plastic knives

Optional
- ❏ *His Name Is John!* Arch Book

Lesson 5

- ❏ Play dough, cookie cutters & dishes
- ❏ Pillow

- ❏ Yarn or ribbon
- ❏ Crackers, cheese & paper plates

Optional
- ❏ Nativity figures
- ❏ *Joseph's Christmas Story* Arch Book
- ❏ Scarves

Lesson 6

- ❏ Yarn & glue sticks
- ❏ Christmas cards
- ❏ Nativity figure of Jesus & gift box
- ❏ Decorating items

Optional
- ❏ Nativity figures & blocks
- ❏ *Baby Jesus Is Born* Arch Book

Lesson 7

- ❏ Hymnals, offering basket & bulletins
- ❏ Decorating supplies
- ❏ Popcorn, oil, salt & popper
- ❏ Paper plates

Optional
- ❏ *Baby Jesus Visits the Temple* Arch Book
- ❏ Baby doll & blanket
- ❏ Glitter or sequins

Lesson 8

- ❏ Art supplies
- ❏ Play dough & star-shaped cookie cutters
- ❏ Flashlight & blue paper
- ❏ Lotion or perfume
- ❏ Candle or incense
- ❏ Gold jewelry
- ❏ Straws & yarn
- ❏ Rickrack or ribbon
- ❏ Zipper bags
- ❏ Star cookies/apples & cream cheese

Optional
- ❏ Paper cups
- ❏ Pan of cornmeal
- ❏ *Star of Wonder* Arch Book

Lesson 9

- ❏ Blocks
- ❏ Hymnals, song sheets, or papers
- ❏ Bible story books

- ❏ Church directory or church picture
- ❏ Paper plates or paint-stirrer sticks
- ❏ Beanbag
- ❏ Pretzels, yarn & napkins

Optional
- ❏ *Jesus and the Family Trip* Arch Book
- ❏ O-shaped cereal
- ❏ Yarn

Lesson 10

- ❏ Dishpan, dishes, detergent
- ❏ Baking items
- ❏ Story bag or paper bag
- ❏ Map
- ❏ Yarn
- ❏ Fruit kabobs/crackers & cheese

Optional
- ❏ Cotton balls

Lesson 11

- ❏ Dishpan of water & seashells
- ❏ Baptismal items
- ❏ Book
- ❏ Yarn & art supplies
- ❏ Tissue paper; ribbon
- ❏ Lemonade mix & water

Lesson 12

- ❏ Small car or toy
- ❏ Graham crackers & tube frosting

Optional
- ❏ *The Story of Jesus' Baptism and Temptation* Arch Book
- ❏ Ribbon or fabric, string, cups
- ❏ Wide satin ribbon, sequins

Lesson 13

- ❏ Puzzles or blocks
- ❏ Toy phone
- ❏ Baby scrapbook, pictures, or items
- ❏ Finger Jell-O children
- ❏ Fish for food

Optional
- ❏ *The Twelve Ordinary Men* Arch Book
- ❏ Craft sticks